OUR FAMILY'S EVOLUTION
From Nationalism to Al-Islam

Abdul Karim Hasan

To my Sister Saida

A.K. Hasan

12-15-19

Our Family's Evolution-
From Nationalism to Al-Islam

Published by BAIT-CAL Publishing

ISBN: 978-0-9859619-2-3

Printed in the United States of America

ABOUT THE AUTHOR

Abdul Karim Hasan was born in 1931 in Camden, New Jersey. He is the seventh of thirteen children.

In 1925, his parents left South Carolina searching for a new, safer and better life than what existed for them as sharecroppers who did not share in the harvesting of the crops.

He was raised by his mother and father who became acquainted with the nationalistic message of the Honorable Marcus Garvey in Philadelphia, Pennsylvania in 1928.

The family moved to Hartford, Connecticut where his mother joined the Honorable Noble Drew Ali's Moorish American Movement in 1942, and enrolled him in their weekend school at the age of eleven.

He grew up in a household environment that preached the historically free and independent life of Africans before slavery, and gravitated towards social movements, following his mother's lead.

His mother heard Minister Malcolm X at a Moorish American Meeting in the summer of 1955. She was fascinated by the message of The Honorable Elijah Muhammad and decided that evening to become a Nation of Islam member. He would join shortly thereafter in 1956.

Rising through the Muhammad Temple of Islam's ranks as Squad Leader, Lieutenant and Acting Captain, he moved to New Haven, Connecticut in 1961 and led the efforts to secure two numbered Temples—Number 40 and 41, in four years as a Minister.

Sent to Los Angeles in 1971, by the Honorable Elijah Muhammad, he led the successful growth in membership and community relations and two years later, purchased a city block at 4016 South Central Avenue, which became Temple #27, the Nation of Islam's West Coast Regional Headquarters.

In 1977, a tribute to his accomplishments was read into the United States of America Proceedings & Debates of the 95th Congress by the Honorable Yvonne Brathwaite-Burke of California.

He would make his first Hajj that same year, while traveling with Imam W. Deen Mohammed, who led a delegation of 300 Americans on Hajj.

He also accompanied Imam W. Deen Mohammed to Rabat, Morocco at the invitation of His Majesty King Hassan II to the Palace to attend the Hassanie Lectures on Hadith during the 1988 Fast and Celebration of the Month of Ramadan."

As an Ambassador of Imam W. Deen Mohammed, he was sent to Rome, Italy to represent Imam Mohammed at an International News Conference.

At the invitation of the President of Egypt, Hosni Mubarak, he was invited to Cairo to receive a Da'wah Medal of Excellence as well as a tour of the City of Qiza, the home of the three internationally recognized Pyramids of the world and the Sphinx, which are classified as wonders of the world, in 1993.

His many travels have carried him to Trinidad-Tobago; Nigeria, Kenya; Malaysia, Singapore; Arabia; Israel; Rome, Egypt; Palestine, Iran, Iraq, Jordan, Syria, and Morocco visiting them many times; making the pilgrimage to Hajj four times and Umra more than a dozen times. He has met and visited with the late

King Khalid of Saudia Arabia, the late Palestinian Authority President Yasar Arafat; and the late Pope John Paul II.

He has prayed in the most Sacred Masajid in the Muslim World including Masjidul Haram (Mecca), Masjidul Nabi (Madina), Masjid At-Taqua (Quba), Majid Al-QiblaTayn (Madina), Masjid Al-Aqsa (Jerusalem), Dome of the Rock (Jerusalem), Masjid Haram Ibrahim (West Bank Palestine), Al-Azhar University (Cairo), and the oldest Masjid in the Kasbah area of Fez, Morocco.

Over the years, he has continued development of the city block at 4016 South Central Avenue with the completion of a 16 Classroom School in 2007; and is currently making progress in the construction of a Masjid and Community Center Complex, at this site. The city of Los Angeles has named this sectional block on Central Avenue at Martin Luther King Blvd and Malcolm X Way, "Imam Abdul Karim Hasan Square."

Table of Contents

ACKNOWLEDGEMENTS

I would like to thank those who have both been essential to this story and in some ways to the completion of this book.

Our grandmother Betty Tention, Toynell Nesmith, Catherene Kelly, Tina Kennedy, Dr. Abdul Majid K. Hasan, Thelma L. McCullough, Edith M. Bowen, David H. McCullough, Donald Bakeer, Mikal Majid, Aisha Abdul Salaam, Joycelyn Rahman, Samir Muqaddin, Lon Muqaddin, and Debra Hasan, who kept insisting I complete the first phase of this book.

This book is dedicated to those three pioneering women from Hartford, Connecticut; Sister Rosalie Beyah, Aunt Pearl Beyah and our mother Larl-El for inviting Minister Malcolm X as the guest speaker at their regular Moorish-American meeting to come back again; the next time to one of their homes. He did return igniting the fire of Islam that would eventually evolve some of their family members into universal Al-Islam. And Sister Martha Peters and her family, who opened her home to us in New Haven that started Islam there.

May Allah forgive them of their faults and mishaps, and accept them into his paradise.

FOREWORD

To the reader

You are about to read a compelling narrative based on historical themes that honor the strength of a family and the spirit of a people. It is written by a man whose life experiences are directly related to the growth of Islam in America. His name is Abdul Karim Hasan.

Hasan uses his literary skills to portray this emotionally riveting story, which begins just after the civil war and goes through some of history's most trying times. His family's challenges on their farm in rural South Carolina and the racism that existed make up the first part of this expose. His mother, who was always seeking knowledge, turned to revolutionary movements to prepare him for his journey over the next seventy years. She provided her family with first-hand information on the Marcus Garvey Movement, Moorish Science Temple and the Nation of Islam.

I first met the author in 1971 after Elijah Muhammad appointed him Minister of Temple #27 in Los Angeles. Soon after his arrival, International trade agreements would bring over a million tons of Whiting fish to Los Angeles. He would supervise distribution to the majority of the country.

In 1974, the author hosted and co-produced the first broadcast of Muslim programming sponsored by Muslim businesses. His guests included Los Angeles Mayor Tom Bradley, Muhammad Ali, Singer Nancy Wilson and actor Brock Peters.

In 1976, the author hosted an international press conference where Imam W. Deen Muhammad, son of The Elijah Muhammad, announced to the world that the Muslim American community was changing from "Black Nationalism to Al-Islam."

In 5 short years I had known him, from 1971-76, he became a significant part of 20th Century Muslim history. Under his leadership, Temple #27 grew from a storefront in South Central L.A. to Masjid Felix Bilal complete with a 1000 student parochial school near downtown Los Angeles.

Thanks to Abdul Karim Hasan's keen depictions of relevant historical data, we have an emotionally riveting story that takes us through the inner workings of the movement. He utilizes photos to lead us through this period in history, and his real-life experiences drive this subject matter into an engaging, compelling story set in the authentic contemporary world of the African American community.

Our company has documented Hasan's travels as a Journalist on behalf of the community to the Vatican, Jerusalem, Palestine, Gaza, Morocco, Saudi Arabia, Malaysia, Mecca and many speaking engagements throughout the United States. Having worked with this author for nearly 50 years, I think I know his credentials.

This is one read you don't want to miss!

Samir Muqaddin
Muslim News Magazine

CHAPTER 1:
Family Life After Slavery

For most people, family history is the primary thread that binds their past, present, and future. Family history shapes the lives of its members for decades, if not centuries and its reverberations create an everlasting story that always plays a role, whether big or small.

These writings are the first-hand account of one such history that represents the extraordinary African-American journey to universal Islam. The story of our family's history begins with our mother's grandfather and grandmother as they evolved from the hardships of slavery, plantation life, and Nationalism to Al-Islam.

Our grandmother said that she, her father, mother, two brothers and her sister lived on a small private farm on the outskirts of Lake City, South Carolina. The year was 1884, nineteen years from the end of the political and economic American Civil War between the Northern Union States and the Confederate (slave) States, and the unintended consequences of freeing enslaved people.

She spoke about how her parents were born in slavery and when the Emancipation Proclamation, issued by President Abraham Lincoln went into effect on January 1, 1863, abolishing slavery in the slaveholding states that were in rebellion, the civil war, which began in South Carolina in April 1861, became fiercer.

The Southerners considered slaves their personal property with ownership rights that couldn't be taken away by the signing of a piece of paper from Washington, DC.

When the Emancipation Proclamation went into effect, the newly freed slaves found themselves caught in the middle. Their new status of freedom left them helpless and homeless. They had no money and no knowledge of how to earn any. They found themselves in a new world, legally denied education in the old world, and now unable to survive on their own. Over the two hundred years of physical slavery, the knowledge of how to survive as an independent human being was lost and erased. They had no concept of freedom, no more than a caged parrot taught how to mimic that word freedom with no sense of what to do when the cage door is left open.

Most of the newly freed slaves, almost to every man and woman, were utterly illiterate. For generation after generation, their whole lives had been spent on the plantation. Slavery was the only life they knew. They were not allowed to go to school, in fact state laws forbade it.

Imagine, millions of people shut-in from the outside world— can't read, can't write, no names to connect them with their ancestors, with no mechanical skills and no language skills. What can they do? Where can they go? How do they connect with the outside world?

Halfway down the road from the only place they called home, many, newly, physically freed slaves got scared and hungry and had to turn around and go right back to the slave master's plantation—begging for food, shelter, and work. The thinkers among the plantation owners invented a new word to fit the new reality, and a new more sophisticated form of slavery entered the lives of millions of displaced ex-slaves —"sharecropper," a system supposedly created to help stabilize the Southern agricultural economy, setting into motion a tenant/plantation owner, business relationship. This new system would allow all ex-slaves to stay on the farm, work the land and share in the profits from the harvested crops. However, the only one profiting from this arrangement was the landowner. Most of the sharecroppers could not read, write or count. They could not keep track of the income and payouts, from their family's labor, which left them at the mercy of the plantation owner's accounting.

Because the Civil War had wrecked the slavery-based economy of the South, our grandmother's father Thomas Tention and her oldest brother, James, who was sixteen at the time, had gone off to Georgia seeking work. During their absence, a significant change was in the works that would tear this family apart and destroy their hope for a future family life together.

On a warm and sunny spring day in 1888, three children, one young nine-year-boy named Henry and two of his sisters, Betty age fourteen and her sister Sarah age eleven, were playing in the front yard of their two-room shack house. The two girls were unaware that two strange men, a white man, and a black man, sitting on a wagon, were watching them.

The so-called white man's name was George B. Nesmith. He lived in Williamsburg County, Township of Turkey, City of Nesmith, South Carolina. When Mr. Nesmith stopped, our great-grandmother Phoebe Tention (spelled on the 1889 U.S. Census as 'Toutan") came out of the house and greeted the strangers. After exchanging words, the man on the wagon (Mr.

Nesmith) told Mrs. Tention that he wanted to take the older girl Bettie with him. On hearing this, Bettie ran off into the woods and hid.

Unable to find her, Mr. Nesmith sent the black man to catch the younger sister Sarah, instead.

Our great-grandmother had witnessed these savage abductions before, where white men just took what they wanted, and she knew that resistance to a white man's wishes, only nineteen years from chattel slavery, was futile. The same law that applied to and protected so-called white people did not apply to ex-slaves or their descendants, especially black women. They knew ex-slaves had no rights that the so-called white man had to accept. He was free to do what he wanted to do, and he often did.

He took eleven-year-old Sarah and carried her to the Township of Turkey, in Nesmith, South Carolina, a farming area, far away from signs of city life where for miles and miles there were only trees, swamps, farming land, and animals to be seen. She was housed in one of his shacks in the middle of acres and acres of land to be farmed and cultivated.

One can only imagine how afraid and alone she was. She was only eleven-years-old. When night came, there was pitch-black darkness. In the daylight hours, all she could see in every direction was snakes, birds, rabbits, squirrels, and vast land. Moreover, when he came to check on her, he would arrive at night and have his way with her and leave.

Fear of what he was capable of doing to her, kept her from running away. Although being a stranger in that area, she had no place to go or hide.

It was several weeks later when Mr. Nesmith appeared again at Mrs. Tention's house demanding the other sister, Bettie—the fourteen-year-old. However, Bettie ran off and hid in the woods, once more.

A few days later Mr. George Nesmith came back and brought two black men with him, and when Bettie ran off again, he told the two black men to run her down and bring her back. They brought her back struggling, crying, and screaming. They threw her into the wagon holding her down while George Nesmith drove away.

Bettie never saw her mother, father, and brother again. However, she did see her sister, Sarah. The two were housed on the same plantation, in different shacks, a considerable distance from each other.

Our mother said that George Nesmith was a very popular landowner, whose extended family was from Scotland. He was married and lived with his family on the plantation. She said, he was also a Methodist minister and a Justice of the Peace.

There were no law or police officers to protect these innocent children taken and forced into a baby-producing factory. Mr. Nesmith was the law. He used a slavery time tactic by changing our grandmother's (Bettie) and her sister's (Sarah) name from their father's former slave master's name, which was Tention (Tanton) to McCutcheon.

Our grandmother was never a McCutcheon. The names used by our great-grandfather and great-grandmother and their children were available on the 1880 United States Census. On that US Census report our great-grandfather is the head of the household.

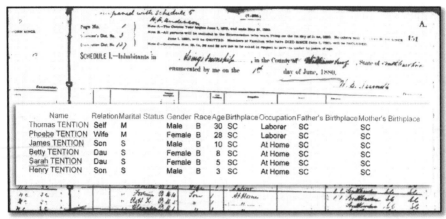

Name	Relation	Marital Status	Gender	Race	Age	Birthplace	Occupation	Father's Birthplace	Mother's Birthplace
Thomas TENTION	Self	M	Male	B	30	SC	Laborer	SC	SC
Phoebe TENTION	Wife	M	Female	B	28	SC	Laborer	SC	SC
James TENTION	Son	S	Male	B	10	SC	At Home	SC	SC
Betty TENTION	Dau	S	Female	B	8	SC	At Home	SC	SC
Sarah TENTION	Dau	S	Female	B	5	SC	At Home	SC	SC
Henry TENTION	Son	S	Male	B	3	SC	At Home	SC	SC

1880 Census

The 1900 US Census list our grandmother as the head of her family and household, with five children, and she spelled her last name Tanton, not McCutcheon.

By the time our mother was born, Mr. George Nesmith had changed her mother Bettie's name to McCutcheon, even though the father of all her mother's seven children (one had died in childbirth) was George Nesmith. Our mother was the seventh child of this relationship, five more were to come after her.

Grandma Bettie's first two children were boys. James was the oldest. He was born according to the 1900 US Census, about 1891 and Benjamin about 1893. Grandma Bettie was about seventeen when James was born. George Nesmith fathered eleven children by our grandmother. On our mother's birth certificate, he is recorded as her father but unmarried to her mother.

The US Census used the word "about" because, in those days, the accuracy of the date of birth of black people was very doubtful due to poorly kept records. The boys were already ten and twelve years old when our mother was born.

Our Grandmother said that when her two boys were very young, they used to talk about never working on the plantation farm of their father.

1900 Census

Both of them were very fair-skinned with features and hair similar to their father and they thought they should have received better treatment from him. However, their father was cruel and unyielding as well as unfriendly toward them. So, they decided to leave South Carolina when they were old enough.

The other children born to our grandmother in the 1890s were: Louise (whom we called aunt Sing), born in 1895, Lottie and her twin sister, both named on the US Census as Lottie. They were born about 1899. With the stillborn child, our grandmother had six children in total by 1901.

Her sister Sarah, according to our mother, had only one child. His name was Ned. Ned and our mother lived in Wilmington, North Carolina but never met each other there.

However, our sister Tina, who also lives in Wilmington, met some of his relatives.

Certificate of Birth

STATE OF SOUTH CAROLINA

COUNTY OF __Williamsburg__

1. PLACE OF BIRTH:
County of __Williamsburg__
Township of __Turkey__
City of __Nesmith__

OFFICE OF CLERK OF COURT

2. FULL NAME OF CHILD: Lawl McCutchen, better known as -- Lawl Nesmith

3. Boy or Girl __Girl__   4. Color or Race __Negro__   5. Nationality __American__

6. DATE OF BIRTH: __July 8, 1904__
(PARENTS ARE NOT MARRIED)   (Month)   (Day)   (Year)

7. Full name __George Nesmith__ FATHER   8. Name before marriage __Bettie McCutchen__ MOTHER

I, __M. S. McFadden__, Clerk of Court of Common Pleas and General Sessions for __Williamsburg__ County, South Carolina, the same being a Court of record, and having by law a seal, and being the official custodian of vital statistics for __Williamsburg__ County, do hereby certify unto all whom it may concern, that pursuant to, and as provided by Act No. 107 of the General Assembly of the State of South Carolina for the year 1939, and as amended, providing for the registration of births of citizens born in said State prior to the year of 1915, there is on record in the office of Clerk of Court for said County the required proof of the birth of the above registrant from which the above statistical data was obtained, and I further certify that the above date of birth, place of birth, and other information concerning the birth of the said registrant is true and correct as copied therefrom.

GIVEN under my Hand and Official Seal of Office at __Kingstree__, South Carolina, this __5th__ day of __May__, A. D. 194__4__.

M. S. McFadden

Clerk of Court for __Williamsburg__ County, South Carolina

By _____ Deputy Clerk.

Our Mother's Birth Certificate

Our mother was born in 1903, and her father George Nesmith acknowledged his parenthood by signing her birth certificate. She was the seventh child of George Nesmith and Bettie Tention (Tanton). Our mother used to share with us the relationship the girls had with their father, which was much, different from that shared with the boys.

Their father had a particular window where he used to sit and read the paper and the Bible, which was in the direction of where the girls lived. The land was flat, and he was able to see anyone coming from across the field.

Being a Methodist preacher, and Justice of the Peace, often on his way to his favorite fishing spot, couples would stop him and ask to be married. He would marry them on the road and tell them to take his note sanctioning the marriage to the courthouse and register.

This religious man, as our mother called him, took two young girls from their mother, fathered thirteen children by them, then expected the children and the mothers to work the land for him as sharecroppers or what amounted to be room and board.

Our mother used to share with us much of the conversation that she had with her mother about Mr. Nesmith when he came for his nightly sexual visits. Her mother said that Mr. Nesmith hated black men, and talked about his hate for them all the time. However, he could not get enough of his sexual encounters with black women.

According to our mother, her mother devised a plan to free herself of him. So, she decided to show him what a Black looked like coming from the same body he liked to use so well and often.

There was this black man who worked in the fields alongside her that she coaxed into having a sexual encounter with her. At first, he was afraid because he knew that she was Mr. Nesmith's woman, and what he would do to him. However, he took a chance, and our grandmother conceived. Of course, the baby boy was born black, and she named him Edward. We called him uncle Ed.

When Mr. Nesmith saw that black baby, he was furious and enraged. Our grandmother said he called her all the nasty and filthy names he could think to say. He ran that baby's father off the plantation threatening to kill him if he ever showed his face in the farming area again.

Instead of putting her off the land too, he said he would disown all the half-white babies she would have after uncle Ed, but he still didn't stop his nightly visits. Mr. Nesmith and grandma Betty had five more babies after uncle Ed, and all of them carried his last name, including uncle Ed.

With high respect for the Christian Bible, nowhere does the Bible say that is okay, or the right thing to do. Moreover, one can imagine this corrupt mentality existed throughout the South for nearly fifteen generations or 300 years.

For three centuries, the Europeans or so-called white landlords and masters exalted themselves as the final evolution of man and the master race, subjecting every other human culture and people as inferior species. In the process, they reduced their human cargo to be their bought slaves, three-fifths of a human in their conscious minds, and property to do with as they pleased. For tax purposes, he called them chattel. Suppose the so-called white people had experienced this cruelty for that long. How would they measure up to today's standards?

The so-called white masters denied their slaves any form of education. In fact, they made it unlawful to teach and educate their human property. Then, they ridiculed them in their storybooks, plays, and theaters as lazy and dumb, even though they did all the work on the plantation, while the master relaxed in the shade of his porch drinking lemonade, made by his slave.

The length of time of controlling people's mind and body established a Southern white superiority culture that has survived until this very day. An idea nourished by table-talk conversations at the old boy's clubs and dinner tables, which acts like a virus, consuming the carrier and infecting the minds of the innocent.

George Nesmith, originally from Scotland, brought into this unique former British Colony of America slaves and so-called white European immigrants, which provided his three families with land taken from the Indians. He had one white family living freely and prosperous, and two half white families living needed and impoverished.

He would be sitting at the window when his daughters used to visit the big house, according to our mother, but they could not go through the fence. They would stop at the section nearest the window, and when he saw them, he would come out and talk to them. Our mother said he used to tell them not to marry black-skinned men, only men of their color. However, they did not accept that advice. All of them married men darker than themselves.

When his white wife would question him regarding the girls coming to the house, our mother said their father would say, speaking of their mother, "That old slut is having another baby." On one occasion our mother said, his wife came out to meet them with a pail half full of milk saying, "Give this to your mother for yawl to drink."

When they got home with the milk, our grandmother told them to go to the barn and pour the milk out. The next day, our mother said there would be a lot of dead rats in the area where they poured the liquid. Mr. Nesmith's wife was not as dumb as he thought; she knew he was fathering all "their" children, and she tried to poison them.

Our oldest sister Toynell said that the hardest working person on the Nesmith farm was grandma Bettie. She used to work the fields from spring to harvest, planting seedlings, cultivating, picking cotton, cutting tobacco and curing it right alongside the children. Not only were the children from this relationship expected to work the farm —in what is now called child labor, but the mother of the children was also supposed to teach and show them how.

No one on the farm was exempt from this laborious task, except the so-called white family. The five or six-year-olds were expected to slop the hogs, milk the cows, feed the chickens, gather straws, sweep the yard and take the cows to the field to graze on the grass. The seven and eight-year-olds were able to stack hay in the barn, clean the animal stalls of manure, chop firewood, help plant corn and tobacco seedling, and irrigate to crops. The nine and ten-year-olds learned how to plow, pick cotton, drive a wagon, suckle tobacco, build tobacco sheds, cure tobacco, cultivate and harvest. There was always something to do on a farm year-round. It was hard work. Every day but Sundays was a working day.

The next two of grandma's daughters to leave Mr. Nesmith's farm was aunt Louise and Lottie, both becoming teenage wives, and eventually moving to Camden, New Jersey.

By 1923, all of grandma Bettie's children had left home except the two youngest ones; Pearl, who was twelve, and Roosevelt (Rose), the youngest, who was ten. The older girls had gotten married and moved away to start their own families. After reaching their teenage years, some of the boys got married and became farmers, while the others followed each other to the North, settling in Philadelphia, Pennsylvania and Camden, New Jersey.

Our Grandma Betty   Aunt Lottie (Honey) and
                             Aunt Louise (Sing)

In the same year, grandma Bettie and her two remaining children (Pearl and Rose), also made plans to move with the help of her children still living in the South and monies sent to her from her sons and daughters in the North.

In 1924, she and her two remaining children hitched the mule to the wagon, loaded all of their personal belongings, and left. Grandma Bettie told us that as they were going, they saw George Nesmith coming down the road riding his favorite white horse. When he saw what they were doing, he gave chase to them. After they reached the main road, he stopped, gave up the chase, and watched them as they rode out of sight.

They arrived late in the evening at one of her daughter's house. Aunt Mattie and uncle Norris were expecting them. They lived in a house in an area with a well-known landmark named, "The Bend in the Road." They never saw George Nesmith again. He died in 1925. He left them some land, but our grandmother never claimed it because it was land infested with rattlesnakes.

CHAPTER 2:
Our Evolution Begins

Our father and mother married in 1919 and hired themselves out to work 50 acres of land as sharecroppers and tenant farmers with the hope of sharing the profits with the plantation owner. For sharecroppers, of course, there were never any or not very much profits to share.

The cruelest word in the English language is said to be, 'almost.' Nowhere was that word more devastating than when said to a sharecropper's family who worked during the fall, winter and spring preparing the land for planting, then, after a spring and summer of hard work: weeding, cultivating, irrigating and praying, the landowner tells them, "Sorry Newtown, you and your family 'almost' broke even this year. Next year should be better." Eventually, our parents said enough is enough. Fed up with this new form of slavery they decided to leave the South.

Our mother had given birth to four children by 1925. The first child was a girl named China, who died as an infant; Nickolas (Nick), Toynell, and Annie Mae.

They left South Carolina for the first time in 1926, leaving our brother Nick and sister Toynell with our grandma Bettie. They took the baby Annie Mae with them and moved to Washington DC, where our father had relatives.

Washington DC in 1926, like almost every other place below the Mason Dixie line, was a difficult place to find work and our father found job opportunities very scarce. He was primarily a farmer and used to putting in work. He could not sit around depending upon his relatives to support him. The city life was destroying him. He started drinking.

Our Father Newton   Our Mother Larl

The reality was he, like many other men trying to escape the South, had no skills that he could adapt for city life. To further complicate an already desperate situation, our mother became pregnant with their fifth child, who was born in 1927. They named her Ruby Lee.

In the spring of 1928, she heard from her brother Mossa, inviting the family to come to Philadelphia and promising them that opportunities were better for them there. As soon as they could, our father and mother with two-year-old Annie Mae and six-month-old Ruby Lee left Washington for Philadelphia, Pennsylvania in late spring. Three of our mother's brothers were there, our uncle James, Benjamin, and Mossa. They had already arranged for an apartment for them.

In this city, "The City of Brotherly Love," is where Mossa, the youngest of the three brothers, introduced our mother, her sister Lottie, and our father to the Marcus Garvey Movement. Also, this is where the evolution of our mother from slavery-time-thinking to Al-Islam began. Her world-view was soon to experience a tremendous change. God is Good!

The city of Philadelphia exposed our family to the invigorating and evolutionary thinking of the Honorable Marcus Garvey and the fledgling world of "Black Nationalism."

Honorable Marcus Garvey   Honorable Duse Mohammed Ali

Marcus Garvey had prepared himself for what he wanted to do in America. He moved from the British controlled island of Jamaica to London, England early in the twentieth century, where he met and exchanged ideas with some of the so-called third world's most progressive and brilliant minds. Among them were Duse Muhammad Ali, Yusuf Abdullah Ali, translator of the Holy

Qur'an; and British convert to Islam and translator of the Holy Qur'an as well as a critical progressive thinker, Professor Muhammad M. Pickthall. However, Duse Muhammad Ali, who followed Garvey to America, was one of Marcus Garvey's most influential associates and had a profound impact on his thinking.

In three years, according to many history writers of that time, Marcus Garvey had amassed a following of over two million black Americans, with over 35 chapters in major cities of America and branches outside America. However, some problems developed among black bourgeoisie and governmental politicians when over two million people were attracted to a black parade in Harlem, New York, which led to charges, convictions and imprisonment of Garvey in 1925. His five year sentence was commuted in 1927, after almost three years in prison, he was deported to Jamaica.

Although many of the chapters remained strong and continued with his message, without a national leader, disunity sat in. However, the Philadelphia chapter, whose members were known as the Philadelphia Garveyites, remained strong and active. Into this chapter, uncle Mossa introduced his siblings and his brother-in-law, our father.

Even though our father did not join, our mother and her sister did and became active members and recruiters. According to our mother, their teachings consisted of good and helpful things. Among them, racial pride; trust in God and the human self; be a good law abiding people; work and save money; raise a race-conscious family; treat every human being with justice and fairness; and, always remember that unity is the key to success. The slogan was, "*One God, One Aim, One Destiny. Up you mighty race, (you can) accomplish what you will.*"

Our mother had finally found something that put her in touch with her feelings and gave her a sense of value, self-worth, and self-esteem. She began to evolve out of that mental complex that inferiority demanded — enforced, by the humiliating culture of the South. She was now starting to think like a free person. Seeing and experiencing a world far different from the one she was raised in, that perpetually placed her life in the position of servitude and disrespect, with very little hope of help coming from Federal, State and Law Enforcement Agencies. That was a law based on seeing black people only as lower-class servants. The North was not that much different, with its housing, business, employment, food establishments biases and other racist practices, but it was a little better than the South.

When our mother attended the first Philadelphia Garveyites' meeting, she became a changed woman, forever. She received a spirit of being and race pride that did not exist in the farm area of the South where she lived. The knowledge of race pride, self-value and self-worth is what she instilled in her eleven surviving children and always taught them to be fair and just. She used to demonstrate to us how they used to exercise and march in the women's auxiliary. She had evolved.

Our mother stayed active for the whole time that she lived in the Philadelphia and Camden, New Jersey area. She gave birth, in 1929, to a son in Philadelphia (Leroy) who died as an infant. Leaving Philadelphia and moving across the Delaware River to Camden, in the summer of 1930, she sent for our brother Nick, sister Toynell, and grandma Bettie to come live with them. All of grandma Bettie's children were grown and married, the youngest girl being aunt Pearl. Roosevelt (Rose), the youngest boy, was killed in a mistaken identity shooting. That was a year before our mother became pregnant with me. However, her pregnancy did not prevent her from attending meetings in Philadelphia and being active in the community.

A discussion developed over naming the new child, boy or girl. Our uncle Mossa was a very knowledgeable person, historically. He was an ardent reader who kept up with world events, especially the struggles taking place in Africa and Asia by the native people that had grown dissatisfied with the rule of the Europeans who, under the ruthless League of Nations, robbed and plundered Africa and Asia of its natural resources with no benefit to them. These were a gang of European so-called white civilized dictators who carved up the black, brown, red, and yellow peoples' land and put themselves in charge of their welfare, politics, economy, and education. In their haste and rush, they carved up areas across tribal areas and named many of these new so-called nations after themselves. They ignored tribal languages and customs that had been established by these people for centuries, thereby, setting into motion war and bloodshed that lasts until this very day.

Our uncle Mossa knew this history, and he followed their struggles in the newspapers and magazines. Being a Garveyite, his world-view was changing. He used to cut out and save all the articles from local newspapers about where and how the struggles for liberation were taking place in Africa. He developed a special attachment for a particular guerrilla leader from Morocco, who had raised a terrific battle against the Spanish, French, and Moroccan Army under French control until he was captured and put in prison. His name was Abd el-Krim, a member of a mountainous ethnic tribe named Rif.

Our uncle so loved the Moroccan leader's exploits that he asked our father and mother that if the baby was a boy, could he name him? They both agreed, and when I was born on September 25, 1931, he named me —Abdel Krim, the English spelling of his name.

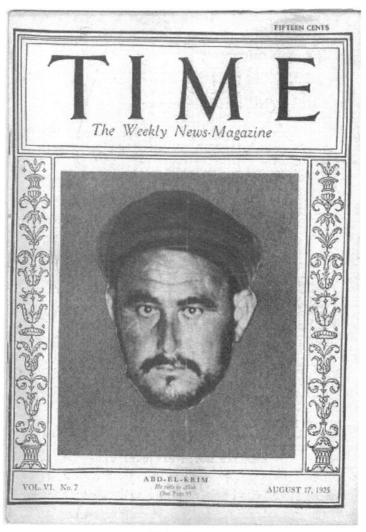

Abd el-Krim
Moroccan Freedom Fighter

I was delivered by a midwife, in a house on the corner of Crescent and Sycamore Street in Camden, New Jersey. Our mother's doctor came later that night, verified the birth and wrote the name as best he could according to the sound.

CHAPTER 3:
North vs. South

In 1932, with the Great Depression in full swing, with joblessness and poverty gripping the city, the effects, and humiliation of proud working people having to wait in soup lines stretching for many city blocks, in many places, were devastating and destructive on city families. Our father was not a lazy man; he worked all his young life, standing in a soup line was out of the question for him. So, our parents decided to move back to South Carolina. Farm work was available there, and a family could grow and raise their food. However, transportation was a problem, and, he had no money and no job.

He told our mother that he was going to this used car lot to see if he could get a car with a promise to pay, later. The used car owner listened to our father's situation very attentively as he explained his predicament with a solemn promise to pay. The owner, an older decent so-called white man, believed our father and said he would trust him. The car was five years old. After signing the agreement papers, our father left.

The very next day our parents loaded what personal belongings they could carry, and with their five children and our grandmother, drove back to South Carolina to the farming town of Kings-tree, to our uncle Norris and our mother's sister, aunt

Mattie's house. They still lived in the same place whose landmark name was "The Bend in The Road."

A few days later, our mother reminded our father that the car he got from that car dealer, on credit, was not paid for, and he must make preparation to return it. Our father agreed and drove the car back to Camden, NJ; returning it to the man who trusted him, explaining that he had moved back to the South, and he could not pay for the car; the man thanked him for his honesty and wished him well.

Type of car our father got on credit in 1932

Our father did not have enough money for the train or bus, and he did not want to beg his relatives for any, so he decided to hitchhike. He said that the first car that came along picked him up. The man was a Caucasian, and it so happened he was on his way to Florida, and our father was welcome to ride with him as far as South Carolina. Nearing South Carolina, he asked our father what city he lived in and offered to take him where he left his family in Kings-tree. He took our father right to the house where he left his wife and family. The family members came out to greet this good Samaritan, offered him food and water, thanked him and wished him well and God's protection on the rest of his journey to Florida. Our father always believed that this man was Jewish.

The next eight years was not an easy time for our father and mother, after living in the North from 1926 to 1932. Their thinking had evolved. However, it took some time to suppress their rejection of the physical and mental abuse of the demeaning culture of the so-called white adult people and their children.

Farm life was a better environment because there was not that many people during the week, only workers. On Saturdays is when most people go to town, and that is where Blacks experienced the most hateful put-downs. Taped on the windows and doors of all the eating-places were signs saying, "No niggers and dogs allowed." There were special windows on the side of the food establishments or in the back where the Black people could get their food, "To Go." It is likely that is where the idea of "Food To Go," which is so prevalent today, got its idea.

The most common name back then for identifying us was not negro but colored, and even the so-called negroes preferred colored more often than negro. However, what we were called depended upon the attitude of who was calling. There were many humiliating and derogatory names used against adults and children too shameful to mention in this writing.

There were two or three farms in the Kings-tree area where our father's family worked the land as sharecroppers. All of them had country stores where the farmers could get their food and supplies on credit. However, most of them were unfair. Landowners kept the records in a book that they called the 'tally book.' At year-end, after the harvesting and sale of the cotton, tobacco, watermelons, and other agriculture products, the landowner and sharecroppers would meet and go over the income and payout for that year. Very few farmers received any income. Almost always they were met with the same storyline. Next year will probably be better, especially if we plant cotton or tobacco in the ten additional acres of the North field. Sometimes it is the South field or West field, but even then, "you almost broke even this year," became heartbreaking and crushing words, especially with every member of a growing family working.

Our mother had three more children in Kings-tree: Edith, Charles Lester, and Thelma, ten family members total, including our mother and father. They say that there were a lot of good white people down there (in the South). Maybe so, but they were silent, afraid to be called "nigger lovers."

In the meantime, our mother grew despondent over not continuing her activities in the Garvey Movement. In Kings-tree, South Carolina, there were no Garveyite type meetings that our mother could attend, only church meetings. Our grandfather was a Founder and Pastor of Saint Marks Methodist Church on the outskirts of Kings-tree, and that is where most of her family and friends attended. So, she started going to our grandfather's church, but not because of spiritual expectations. She needed social connections, and she found that in the company of her family and friends there.

I was six years old when she started taking our sister Feedie and me with her to church. At church meetings when the hostess came by, she would give me a penny to drop in the collection tambourine. Our mother was teaching how important it was to be charitable. We sat there beside her anxiously waiting for the hostess, and, when she came, putting that penny in the collection tambourine was a big moment.

For the Easter Stage Play, my older sister Toynell, use to dress me in a paper outfit she made so I could participate in the children's Easter Program. She even wrote the words that I would say and taught me to memorize them. Those words are still remembered 80-years later:

> "What are you looking at me
> So hard for? I didn't come
> To stay. I just came to tell
> you, the day is Easter Day."

The social connection among these poor black dirt farming church going people was a one-day relief from the harsh reality of denial and cruelty in South Carolina. However, having a small taste of freedom in the North, it was time for our family to move on.

Our father and mother made a conscious decision that it was time to leave the place of their birth. Our mother's youngest sister, Pearl, and her husband Otis Syms had left the South several years before and had established themselves in Hartford, Connecticut. They kept writing them telling them how much better living conditions were in Hartford, and they should come. They convinced our parents that jobs were available and affordable housing was near where they lived.

The year that migration began was in 1940, about eighteen months before the beginning of World War II. Our father went first. He found a job in a foundry, paying forty dollars a week.

He found an apartment in a three-story, six-unit apartment building at Number 8 Donald Street.

Meanwhile, our grandfather sent uncle Andy to the landowner's plantation to move us to his land on the far side of Kings-tree. Uncle Andy had just built a new house out of pinewood, and memories of that pine scent are still captured today.

Our brother Nick and sister Toynell were living in Columbia, South Carolina where they were finishing high school. There were no high schools in Kings-tree that Black people could attend through the eleventh and twelfth grades. Secondary schools only went to the tenth grade. They attended Booker T. Washington High School while working for wealthy people as maid and chauffeur.

Six children were left with our mother in uncle Andy's new house until our father sent for our mother and the three youngest children (Edith, Charles Lester, and Thelma). Annie Mae, 14-years old, Ruby Lee 12-years old and I, eight years old, were left with our grandparents, we worked in the fields until our mother wrote our sister Toynell, in Columbia and told her to pick us up and take us to her sister aunt Mattie and her husband, uncle Norris's farm.

Months passed until our father's friends, who were going to Florida, were paid by him to pick us up from our aunt and uncle's house on their return. During the trip, we stopped for gas and were not allowed to use the toilets. Instead, the women had to go behind the station into the woods to relieve themselves. We did not experience that problem in South Carolina, because blacks and whites seldom mixed.

However, there are memories of playing with the plantation owner's two children at the age of six or seven years old. Then strangely, something happened to change that. Mr. George Bar, the plantation owner, came home one day while us children were playing in the yard with their toys —like we always did, Mr. Bar told me not to come back over to his house again. After telling our mother what he said, she said, "Well, don't go back over there." That is all she said, and I never did.

CHAPTER 4:
Discovering Our Identity

So, this thing with black people is cultural, and it runs deep because we did nothing to so-called white people to deserve it. We did not kill their soldiers in war, we did not destroy their farmland and home, we did not assault and abuse them, and we did not rape their women, as they did ours. We did not ride against them at night, burning crosses soaked in gasoline, killing men, women, and children as they were fleeing from the fire. We did not shame them before the world with Hollywood films depicting them as lazy, slothful, ignorant and nincompoops, maids, butlers, clowns, and buffoons in movies. No! We served them faithfully as their property for nearly 300 years.

Moreover, if that was not enough humiliation for those Southerners and Northern soldiers, during World War I, World War II, and the Korean Conflict, they took their hate with them; spreading lies on black soldiers, calling them monkeys with tails. They set up white-soldiers-only bars in foreign countries making it off limits for the black soldiers who were fighting and dying for freedom, justice, equality, and the American Way!

Hollywood, the American center and entertainment capital of the world, could have done much more, to tell the truth. Instead, they choose to lie and distort the lives and habits of millions of

African-Americans all for the all mighty dollar, at the global expense of Black Patriotic Americans.

Just look at how they depicted the American Indians, the Asian Indians, the South American Indians and the Africans. Lily-white Tarzan, the King, and Lord of the Jungle, as he swung on the vine, jumping from tree to tree, hollering like a wild man with elephants following him, lions stopping in their tracks, and the poor Africans shaking and trembling like leaves on trees in the wind. He ends up beating up hundreds of fearful natives while saving the day.

Movies depicted Frank 'bring em back alive' Buck, standing firm in the path of a charging wild beast, while the African supply carriers threw off their baggage and started running. These same Africans had to prove their manhood by facing lions with only a spear.

We will not mention, The Phantom "the ghost who walks", Sheena of the Jungle, or Jungle Jim. There was not an African hunter or brave person to be seen on the movie screen, anywhere!

Hollywood has been the destroyer of millions of people's minds, characters, and customs.

In this type of environment, produced by Hollywood, is where this author grew up. A lily-white world of saviors filmed in Hollywood; put on nationwide screens as entertainment, subliminally seducing us, while we pay for it.

No one is lily-white in the context of religious concept and interpretation. White means "pure," not human. In religious interpretation and concept, black means— spiritual darkness. There are no pure human beings and no white human beings. Pink may be a better word.

These color distinctions were used to divide people. Asians do not call themselves, yellow people. Enlightened Europeans do not call themselves, white people. North American Indians do not call themselves, red people. South American people do not call themselves, brown people. It is hard to imagine that Africans ever called themselves, black people. Why? Because the land, language, and culture from which they came, is what identified them.

The Hollywood writers are super intelligent. They know the world history of myth, science, cultures, languages, customs, and religions. They know when they are falsifying history and making a satire of people's lives. Also, so do the film directors, the producers and big studio companies who do not care. All they want is to make money. They could have given the so-called Black-Americans a better image. After all, they gave themselves a better, underserved image.

It was in Hartford, Connecticut in 1941, at the age of nine-years-old, fresh out of Kings-tree, South Carolina when I saw my first motion picture. Within two years, I was screaming, clapping, and hollering for the British controlled soldiers of India to save them from the Indian people seeking independence or the cavalry to save the wagon train from the so-called savages. Watching Tarzan rescuing a handful of people from five-thousand frightened, wide-eyed Africans and the Phantom, the savior of white people from jungle people, and, a lily-white man, hanging from two pieces of wood — the savior of the world.

Hollywood sold these stories to the world and the world bought it. All for money, control, and the power to be "savior of the world," by suppression, oppression and the idea that, "might makes right."

33

However, in 1942 my thinking and mental evolution began to change when our mother and aunt Pearl discovered the message of the Moorish Science Temple and the Honorable Noble Drew Ali, its Leader and Founder.

Honorable Noble Drew Ali

Our father met a man on his job, whose name was Brother Coleman 'Bey'. He was a member of the Moorish Science Temple in Hartford. Brother Coleman tried to persuade my father to come to one of their meetings. Although our father was not interested, he did tell Brother Coleman that he would invite him to his home and introduce him to his wife and family who like his kind of message.

Our father was not a joiner of anything, but he had no objections to our mother listening and joining if she liked. Our mother and aunt Pearl accepted an invitation to visit the Moorish American Temple and were very impressed, so they joined. When the Temple moved from Village Street to Main Street and established a weekend school, I attended every weekend.

Our family was given the "El," to wear after our slave-name to denote that we were Moorish, descendants from the original inhabitants of Morocco (also know as Moors) who were the people that sailed off to Spain with Islamic enlightenment. Our aunt Pearl and her family received the designation of 'Bey.'

Our Sunday school teacher was Sheikh F. Turner-El. He used to teach our weekend school class. He was a big man with a crystal clear, distinctive, loud booming voice, and he would get the classes attention and keep it until class was over.

Group of Moorish American Teachers,
Sheikh F. Turner-El (far left)

I used to wear a red fez to and from our meetings and was proud of that fez. It made me feel important. Learning something about Muslim heritage that I never knew before. It was a new language and new thinking for me and my sisters, brothers, and friends in our neighborhood.

The Moorish Americans taught that they were the successors of the Marcus Garvey Movement, which thrived in the New Haven and Hartford, Connecticut area at that time. They were good people, family people, and business people who owned a variety of different business serving the community. As a group, they bought many acres of land in Great Barrington, Massachusetts that we used to visit often for special meetings and social events.

Our oldest brother Nick, who was twenty-three, borrowed money from our mother and bought a grocery store on Russell Street, which was being sold by this Jewish family. The neighborhood was in the midst of changing from so-called white to black, and it was in an excellent location. Nick's wife Wilhelmina operated the store through the week while he worked at the Colt Manufacturing Company. Because he was a smart businessman at such a young age, he was asked to chair the Business Group.

It was here that we received early training in business. Through the younger teenage years, we worked and learned the grocery business from our brother Nick, after school and on weekends. My younger brother Charles Lester (Dr. Abdul Majid K. Hasan) received business training from the grocery store, as well. By the age of fourteen, we could operate and manage the store.

A Jewish grocer taught us how to place the grocery items in the paper bag. He said, heavier ones first. There were no adding machines in general use in those days; each column of numbers had to be added by head, hand, and pencil.

As kids, we kind-of-strayed somewhat from attending the Moorish Science Temple meetings, but our mother and aunt Pearl did not. They attended weekly meetings while the rest of us only went to special events. However, we never gave up our belief, relationship, and connection with the Moorish American boys and girls our age.

Eventually, our brother's family business expanded to include a Dry Cleaning Plant in our mother's building, and another Dry Cleaning Plant and Shirt Laundry at another site, employing our sisters Feedie, Thelma, and Tina. The Dry Cleaning and Laundry included pickup and delivery services. I used to clean the clothes, spot the clothes, and press the clothes. I had three skilled professions before I was twenty-three: professional photographer; darkroom film developer; and, business management.

Married to my teenage girlfriend Eloise, we raised a son, Kenneth, who eventually went to Connecticut State College, Yale University, and Antioch College in Yellow Springs, Ohio. We owned two cars, and in partnership with our mother and brother Charles, we bought a three-family house. Living was good. Charles and I had a plan to buy more houses next door to each other until we owned all the apartments on the block. We planned to become "rich" through ownership of rental property.

Great idea, we thought, but it all changed. Our family was on the brink of making another evolutionary change.

CHAPTER 5:
A Nation Calls

In 1955 our mother and her sister, aunt Pearl were attending a regular Moorish American meeting, when they learned that they had a guest speaker that night.

The Grand Sheikh had invited a young minister from Temple #7 Harlem, New York to be the main speaker for the evening. It was a Thursday night. The young minister's name was Malcolm X. He was 30 years old.

Our mother said that this young minister's message was so powerful, straightforward, and dynamic that she and others wanted to hear him again. Some of the members asked the Sheikh to invite Minister Malcolm X back again. The Sheikh said, "No! Malcolm X would steal all our followers."

So, sister Rosalie "Bey," my aunt Pearl "Bey," and our mother talked to Minister Malcolm X afterward and asked him would he come back if they invited him. He said, "Yes," if they would invite their families and friends to one of their homes, he would be pleased to come back.

True to his word, Minister Malcolm X came back to a packed living room, and the original invitees stood up and asked him how they could become Temple of Islam members. Minister Malcolm X showed them how, and the process to become registered members began.

No one joined the Muhammad's Temples' Nation of Islam. Member candidates had to write a letter following exact instructions, and then wait to see if the letter passed the national laborer's inspection. Membership required sincerity. Passing the difficulty of writing that letter took sincerity, patience and time.

Letter for Nation of Islam Membership

The letter read, in part:
"Dear Saviour Allah, Our Deliverer..."

The punctuation had to be precisely the same as the letter. Dotted I's, crossed T's, single back T's, loops in the L's, single back D's. It was not easy for some people.

If the letter passed inspection, they received a letter acknowledging their acceptance and informing them to go the

Secretary and get the number of their X.

Members were given an X after their given name. The message was that the first name was the given name, and the last name came from the final slave master that owned an individuals ancestors during and after slavery was abolished. Therefore, placing the X after their given name meant they no longer accepted that last name, nor recognized it as a family name because it was not the name of their African ancestor. It is the name of the last slave master before Emancipation.

If two people had the same name, the first member received an X, the second 2X. For example, the first John would be named John X, and the second John would be named John 2X. It was the same process for those with initials.

Minister Malcolm X answered questions and promised to come back if they invited new people to the next meeting.

Our mother was on fire. With 11 children living, and half of them married, she did not let any of us rest. All she wanted us to do was come one time, that is all. One time and we would not have to come anymore. My wife, Eloise, couldn't take it anymore, so she went. She came back on fire. Now, we had two people pressing us day and night.

Our mother owned this three-family house, and we rented the first floor, so I saw her every day. "You have got to come and hear Minister Malcolm X. You have got to come and hear Minister Malcolm X," she would say. However, I resisted, quietly. After all, that was our mother, and I loved and respected her.

In February 1956, our mother went to Chicago for the Annual Moslem Convention, which in later years changed its name to the Saviour's Day Convention. At this convention, she saw and heard the Honorable Elijah Muhammad speak. For five days she was gone, and when she came back, she was more excited than before she went. So, to satisfy our mother's continuous, round the clock persistence once and for all, I agreed, along with some of my brothers and sisters, to go with our mother to hear this Minister Malcolm X.

The meeting was on a cold Thursday night during the first week in March 1956. In just nine months the attendance had outgrown all the members' houses, and the meetings now held at the North-End Community Center on North Main Street in a complex owned by an African American.

As I walked through the door, the secretary took my name and commented that it was a Muslim name. I did not comment. I was immediately ushered into the room and seated in the front row. The hall, full of chairs smartly lined, filled up quickly.

At precisely seven o'clock a member of Minister Malcolm X's student ministers' class, Assistant Minister Thomas JX opened the meeting: As-Salaam-Alaikum, the Minister said. "Would you all please rise and face the East. We are going to begin our meeting with a prayer." He called it the Opening Prayer. He recited this prayer in English from memory:

"Surely I have turned myself to Thee, O Allah. Trying to be upright to He who originated the heavens and the earth. And, I am not of the polytheists.

"Surely my prayer and my sacrifice, my life, and my death are all for Allah, the Lord of the Worlds.

"No associates has He and of this am I commanded. I am of those who submit.

"O Allah, Thou art the King; there is no God but Thou. Thou art my Lord and I am Thy servant.

"I have been greatly unjust to myself, and I confess my faults. So grant me protection against all my faults. For none grants protection against faults but Thou.

"And guide me to the best of morals for none guides to the best of morals but Thou.

"And turn away from me the evil and indecent morals for none can turn away from me the evil and indecent morals but Thou.

"Oh Allah, make Muhammad successful and the followers of Muhammad successful here in the wilderness of North America, as Thou did make Abraham successful and the followers of Abraham. For surely Thou art Praised and Magnified.

"Oh Allah, Bless Muhammad and the followers of Muhammad here in the wilderness of North America, as Thou did Bless Abraham and the followers of Abraham. For surely Thou art Praised and Magnified. Amen."

After the prayer, we were asked to sit down, and the Assistant Minister began to explain the meaning of "As Salaam Alaikum" and "Wa Alaikum Salaam."

He spoke for about fifteen minutes welcoming the people and also explaining various Arabic words that we would be hearing in Minister Malcolm X's lecture, like "Allah," "Islam," "Muhammad," "Qur'an," "Mecca," and others.

Minister Thomas JX then introduced Malcolm X as the Minister of Temple #7 Harlem, New York, sent there by the Honorable Elijah Muhammad.

Malcolm X was converted to the message of the Nation of Islam while serving a ten-year sentence in a Massachusetts State Prison, which began in 1945, for burglary. He was 20 years old. Ironically, the same year that Malcolm was entering prison, the Honorable Elijah Muhammad was being released from Federal Prison for the crime of refusing to register for the World War II draft.

Malcolm X had four brothers. Three of them were members of the Nation of Islam, and they would write and visit him. His oldest brother, Wilfred, wrote him every week. However, it was his brother Reginald, who became secretary of Temple #7, who used to visit him the most.

According to Malcolm X's brother Wilfred, whom I knew very well; it was Reginald whose visit with Malcolm that persuaded him to study the message of the Honorable

Elijah Muhammad and consider becoming a Muslim. He told Malcolm about the Nation of Islam's teachings. That white men collectively were devils, and the black men collectively were gods, who had been put to sleep for 6,000 years. Now, it was time to wake up and reclaim their own. The black race is a member of the black, brown, red and yellow people, and much more than that.

After hearing these things and more from his brother Reginald, Malcolm X's mind went into research mode. He wanted to search history to see if there was any relevance of truth to what his brother was telling him. Malcolm did something that he had never done before. He went to a prison library and began to read every book of related subjects that would prepare him to preach and defend the Honorable Elijah Muhammad and the Nation of Islam. He had converted.

From books, Malcolm X said he discovered the shockingly brutal acts committed upon third world people of India, China, Africa, South and Central America, and the Islands of the Pacific by Europeans. Any other way could not describe these criminal acts than acts by devilish men.

Mr. W. D. Fard taught the new members in Detroit that the white race was a race of devils that did devilish things to the non-European people. In his search, Malcolm X learned of the Boxer Rebellion in China, when Chinese people rose up against the British who were forcing opium upon their people, that the battle cry was, "Kill the foreign white devils." The date was at the beginning of the twentieth century, 30-years before Mr. W. D. Fard started teaching that the white man is the devil to the members of the Nation of Islam and 80-years before Ayatollah Khomeini called America the 'big devil.'

Malcolm X said that he spent days and nights in prison reading and studying books. Some of the books he read were:

- Will Durant's, Story of Civilization
- H. G. Wells, Outline of History
- W. E. B. Du Bois, Souls of Black Folks
- Carter G. Woodson's, Negro History
- J. A. Rogers, Three Volumes of Sex and Race, AESOP and his fables, Egypt's Pharaoh, and Great Coptic Christians
- New York Times articles by noted author, Arnold Toynbee
- Gregor Mendel, Finding Genetic Empires: Ethiopia (ancient Abyssinia) the country where the Negus gave refuge to the eighty fleeing Muslims (including the Prophet's daughter, Ruqayyah) who sought and were given protection by them.

Malcolm X once said, "I never will forget how shocked I was when I began reading about slavery's total horror. It made such an impact upon me that it later became one of my favorite subjects when I became a minister of the Honorable Elijah Muhammad. The world's most monstrous crime, the sin and blood on the so-called white man's hands is almost impossible to believe".

Over 100,000,000 Africans, according to historian J. A. Rogers, were uprooted from Africa and scattered throughout the Western Hemisphere. These merchants of death brought and sold human beings in America, Haiti, Brazil, Cuba, Trinidad, Tobago, East Indies, West Indies, Puerto Rico, Bermuda, and on and on. However, the most brutal were in North America, excluding Canada (who were humane Christians).

Fresh out of prison, Malcolm X wrote his letter applying for membership in the Nation of Islam, and it was accepted. Traveling to Chicago with his brother, Wilfred, he soon met the Honorable Elijah Muhammad, whom he had written every day while in prison. He traveled back and forth from Detroit to the Chicago, the home of the Honorable Elijah Muhammad for private teaching and guidance.

Minister Malcolm X
(el-Hajj Malik el-Shabazz)

Malcolm X rose quickly through the ranks of Detroit's Temple #1 becoming assistant minister to Minister Lemuel Hassan, less than one year out of prison.   Because he was an activist, Malcolm X brought more people to Temple meetings than all the other brothers combined. Moreover, because of this,

Temple Number One's attendance tripled in less than three months.

The Honorable Elijah Muhammad saw promise in Malcolm and Malcolm's desire to help him open Temples in every small and major city in America. He decided to send him where he could help the most, the East Coast. Malcolm X's first assignment was in Boston, Massachusetts. He began teaching in the living room of a brother named Lloyd X who was a musician. Later, Brother Lloyd became the minister of Springfield, MA, Temple #13 and our minister at Temple #14 in Hartford, CT.

In three months, they had grown out of the house and into a storefront with a Temple address. Malcolm's next assignment was in Philadelphia where the meetings were in another house. Again, within a few short months, they had grown out of the house and into a storefront with a Temple address.

From Philadelphia, the Honorable Elijah Muhammad sent Malcolm X to Harlem, New York's Temple #7. In Harlem, New York, Malcolm X felt that he had finally made it to his place in history. The year was 1954; Malcolm X was only 29 years old. There were only eight numbered Temples at that time in our history: Detroit, Chicago, Milwaukee, Washington DC, Cincinnati, Baltimore, Harlem, and San Diego. By 1956, the Nation of Islam had added two additional Temples; Temple #9 Akron and #10 Atlantic City, however, it was clear there was much more work to do. So Minister Malcolm X, who was a tireless worker, led the charge.

In 1956, Minister Malcolm X was appointed by the Honorable Elijah Muhammad as his National Spokesman for the Nation of Islam.

After his introduction that night, the first Thursday in

March 1956 at the North-End Community Center, Hartford, CT, Minister Malcolm X spoke to a packed house of over 100 people. He greeted us with, 'Salaam Alaikum,' and then he flipped over a blackboard and began talking.

The Blackboard Message

Malcolm X's message that night was mesmerizing. He held his audience riveted as he retold the history of black people captured in Africa, kidnapped, brought to America, South America, and the Caribbean Islands by the British, Portuguese, Dutch, French, and the Spanish; sold into slavery to plant, grow and harvest cotton, sugar cane, tobacco, cocoa, and more. He went on to teach that Mr. W. D. Fard (who also used the name Mr. W. F. Muhammad, and Mr. Wallace D. Fard) had a plan. He also said (W. D. Fard) taught the Honorable Elijah Muhammad that the first captives brought to America were in 1555, and not in 1619, aboard an English ship, captained by a Sir

John Hawkins. The name of the ship was, "Good Ship Jesus." They were Christians. None of the captives, however, were Christians. Many were Muslims. The name of our G-d was Allah. Our Holy book was the Qur'an, and our religion was Islam. With the words and images on the blackboard and his explanations, we were all spellbound.

This was my first meeting, and I was there as a guest of our mother and my wife, Eloise. I had never heard anything as mentally uplifting as those talks Malcolm X gave. Where could I have gone to hear a message like this? Nowhere! Indeed, not in schools and not in social meetings. Not in book clubs, not in movies. It was a history that changed the course of my life.

When Minister Malcolm X was finished with the question and answer session, and there were many, if you were not convinced during his talk, the answer to every question most certainly was convincing. The most engaging questioner was a young Holiness Minister, with a Bible in his hand. Minister Malcolm X dispatched him with such finesse that the young minister sat down with no more questions and soon left.

With no more questions, Minister Malcolm X asked, "How many of you are here for the first time. Please raise your hands and stand up." I stood up along with many others.

"How many of you standing believe that what you heard is the truth?" My hand went up as did many others.

"How many of you who believed that what you have heard is the truth, would like to accept this truth?" My hand went up again and many others. Minister Malcolm X said, "You have made the right choice. Please follow this Brother and he will take you to the secretary who will explain to you the procedures."

I could hear my mother chuckle in the background, pleased by the fact that her son finally accepted the message that she had been trying to teach them ever since she heard it. It is what she had hoped for.

Minister Malcolm X then closed out the meeting with a prayer. He called it a Closing Prayer:

> "In the Name of Allah, The Beneficent, The
> Merciful. All praise is due to Allah the Lord of all the
> Worlds. The Beneficent, The Most Merciful, Master of
> this day of judgment in which we now live. Thee alone
> do we serve and to Thee alone do we beseech for aid.
> Guide us along the right path. The path of those upon
> whom Thou has bestowed favors, not of those upon
> whom Thy wrath is brought down nor of those who go
> astray after they have heard Thy teaching. "Say He Allah
> is One God. Allah is He of whom nothing is
> independent but upon whom we all depend. He neither
> begets nor is He begotten and none is like Him. "And, I
> bear witness that none deserve to be served besides Allah,
> and I bear witness that The Honorable Mr. Elijah
> Muhammad is his true servant and apostle. Amen."

Before dismissal, Minister Malcolm X and every minister in the Nation of Islam repeated these instructions from the Honorable Elijah Muhammad.

"Islam means peace, so seek peace. Never be the aggressor, but if anyone attacks you, we don't teach you to turn the other cheek. May Allah bless you to be successful and victorious in all that you do. As-Salaam Alaikum."

51

However, it was not the religion that impressed me. It was the information, the militancy, and the courage. Religion was not being taught, but the knowledge of self was.

CHAPTER 6:
Answering The Call

I wrote my letter for membership in the Nation of Islam in March 1956, and I received my letter of acceptance from the National Laborers in Chicago dated April 6, 1956, along with my first two lessons: Student Enrollment Rules of Islam and Actual Facts.

I was directed to go see the Temple Secretary and get the number of my X. All incoming members were considered students and all were required to study and memorize the Morning Prayer (also called the Opening Prayer) and other lessons.

Honorable Elijah Muhammad

Mr. W. D. Fard

Mr. W. D. Fard gave these mythical and mystic lessons to the Honorable Elijah Muhammad in the early 1930s. Each lesson had to be memorized and recited in the presence of a Temple official before advancing to the next lesson. There were five lessons, plus the Opening and Closing Prayer and Actual Facts.

The first lesson new members completed was called "Student Enrollment Rules of Islam." The other lessons were "Lost Found Moslem Lesson #1," "English Lesson C#1," "Lost Found Moslem Lesson #2," and the "Problem Book." What follows is an excerpt of English Lesson C#1, which included thirty-six questions, statements, and answers on one typed page.

1. My name is W. F. Muhammad.
2. I came to North America by myself.
3. My uncle was brought over here by the Trader three hundred seventy-nine years ago.
4. My uncle cannot talk his own language.
5. He does not know that he is my uncle.
6. He likes the devils because the devil gives him nothing.
7. Why does he like the devil?
8. Because the devil put fear in him when he was a little boy
9. Why does he fear now, since he is a big man?
10. Because the devil taught him to eat the wrong food
11. Does that have anything to do with the above question? ANSWER: No! Number 10?
12. Yes, sir, that makes him other than his own self.
13. What is his own self?
14. His own self is a righteous Muslim

15. Are there any Muslims other than righteous?

16. I beg you pardon, I have never heard of one

17. How many Muslim sons are there in North America

18. Approximately three million.

19. How many Original Muslims are there in North America?

20. A little over seventeen million

21. Did I hear you say that some of the seventeen million do not know that they are Muslims?

22. YES SIR.

23. I hardly believe that, unless they are blind, deaf and dumb.

24. Well, they were made blind, deaf and dumb by the devil when they were babies.

25. Can the devil fool and Muslim?

26. NOT-NOW-ADAYS.

27. Do you mean to say that the devil fooled them three hundred seventy-nine years ago?

28. Yes, the Trader made an interpretation that they receive GOLD for their labor, more than they were earning in their own country.

29. Then, did they receive gold?

30. No! The Trader disappeared and there was no one that could speak their language.

31. Then what happen?

32. Well, they wanted to go to their own country; but they could not swim 9,000 miles.

33. Why didn't their own people come and get them?

34. Because their own people did not know that they were here.

35. When did their own people find out that they were here?

36. Approximately 60 years ago.

None of the lessons were designed to teach the religion of Al-Islam, but rather to clean up the mind and body; develop discipline; courage; self-confidence; self-respect; self-reliance; knowledge of self and build a close brother and sister relationship that said, "You can count on me."

All African-Americans were classified as members of the Tribe of Shabazz, Lost Found Members of the Nation of Islam and were students of Mr. W. D. Fard, a man who came to America from the Pakistani area of India, who said that he was from the Holy City of Mecca, Arabia.

It was Mr. W. D. Fard who also introduced himself as Wallace D. Fard. It was W. D Fard who said he was a prophet, and it was he who described a prophet as one who came to uplift fallen humanity, which were the very words and language used by Noble Drew Ali, Moorish American founder and leader around the turn of the twentieth century.

In English Lesson #C1 — Mr. W. D. Fard introduced himself as W. F. Muhammad, who came to North America by himself.

It was Mr. W. D Fard who taught that Africans were brought here (to America) by the slave traders and deprived of all knowledge of their past. And, that there was no way of any help coming to us, nor did help come to us until the coming of the son-of-man in the person of himself, W. D. Fard.

When Mr. W. D. Fard used the term son-of-man, the Honorable Elijah Muhammad, who was a student of the Bible, said he understood him to be like Christ Jesus or (as most western Christians believe) God in human flesh. However, Mr. W. D. Fard did not teach that he was the son-god, manifested.

This new language: Allah, Muhammad, Islam, Muslim, As-Salaam-Alaikum, Madhi, came directly from the lessons, workbooks, and assignments to the member-students of the Nation of Islam, under Mr. W. D. Fard.

For three and one-half years he taught this message in Detroit, Michigan; Chicago, Illinois; and in Milwaukee, Wisconsin. Mr. W. D. Fard founded Temple #1 in Detroit. Also, he and the Honorable Elijah Muhammad founded Temple #2 in Chicago and Temple #3 in Milwaukee.

Mr. W. D. Fard left the Honorable Elijah Muhammad with the tremendous task and responsibility of taking the message to the people. His mission was to build the African-American Muslim Community into a Nation. However, first, he must reform them.

The Honorable Elijah Muhammad told Malcolm, when Malcolm received his X, "Go after the young men, that will shame the older men and that if you can attract the young women, they will attract the young men."

During our orientation classes in Hartford, Connecticut, we learned about the F.O.I (Fruit of Islam) and the M.G.T & G.C.C (Muslim Girl Training, General Civilization Class).

These were separate classes of men and women who belonged to Islam in North America, initially established by Mr. W. D. Fard. All men and women coming into The Lost Found Members of the Nation of Islam automatically became an M.G.T or F.O.I, regardless.

Each class had individual officials, captains, lieutenants, and secretaries. Originally, in Connecticut and other Temples in the Nation, the F.O.I would meet on Monday nights and the M.G.T on Tuesday nights. Later, after the death of President John F.

Kennedy, the two classes were changed to Saturday in the daytime. The men and women would meet jointly, only at public meetings - Wednesday nights, Friday nights, Sunday at 2 p.m., and Temple Laborers' meetings.

Our orientation class introduced us to the "Do's and the Don'ts."

- No pork or its by-products
- No alcoholic beverages, liquors, wines, beer
- No illegal drugs, hashish, marijuana
- No tobacco products, snuff, chewing tobacco, cigars, cigarettes, cigarillos

We were not to buy, use, nor sell these products in our stores and businesses.

- No weapons, no pistols, rifles or shotguns on your person or in homes. Allah is our weapon.
- No gambling, cards for money, dice, policy numbers, checkers, sweepstakes or any games of chance. No betting of any kind.

There were lists of twenty instructions on how we should conduct ourselves. Disobeying any of the instructions carried a penalty of expulsion for at least 90 days from Temple activities.

There was another list called — "Restricted Laws of Islam." Thirty-five additional rules to believe, memorize and obey. They were the Do's. They were simple. Some of those rules were:

- Fear no one but Allah.
- Obedience to the Messenger is obedience to Allah, as the Messenger is the bearer of Allah's message.
- Keep up prayer.
- Spend of what Allah has given you in the cause of Islam.

- Love your brother believer as yourself.
- Be kind and do well to all.
- Do unto others as you would want done unto you.
- Obey those in authority among you and obey non-believers in authority over you as long as it does not conflict with your religion.
- Always work for unity.
- It is forbidden to commit fornication or adultery
- It is forbidden to commit indecent acts on another (sodomy).
- Do not feel, rub or pat sisters.
- Do not stare at sisters or watch movements of their body.
- No slack talk (negative comments about others).
- No gossip
- Do not deal with hypocrites or show sympathy toward them.
- Do not lust
- Must be clean at all times (mind and body) at home and abroad.
- No lying (speak the truth regardless of circumstances).
- No stealing
- Do not commit acts of violence on others or ourselves.

All of these things and more were part of orientation for the brothers and sisters.

During the orientation sessions, I received my introduction to the F.O.I Class. The first mentioning of the F.O.I Class is found in Lesson #1, number 12, question and answer:

What is the meaning of F.O.I?

Answer: The "Fruit of Islam" the name given to the military training of the men and boys who belong to Islam in North America.

The Nation of Islam taught that a "Fruit" is the best! He is continually training and conditioning himself to meet and overcome all obstacles in his path. His sole purpose is to deliver the seventeen million (and more) dead to the Lamb of God, the Honorable Elijah Muhammad.

To do this meant that we had to learn how to approach our people with this new idea and new language.

At the start of my orientation, I went to my first F.O.I meeting. The F.O.I meeting was in Harlem, New York, at Muhammad's Temple #7.

We agreed to meet at my house at 5:00 p.m. to car-pool to New York. I drove my car because it was new, and New York was 120 miles from Hartford.

I always had a car because I always worked. I bought my first car in partnership with my best friend Aaron Hosendove, whom I first met in elementary school, in the 5th grade. We bought the car when we were both seventeen, and too young to register the car. His mother registered it for us. The year was 1949. It was a 1936 Ford, and we paid $35.00 for it. I had to buy and install a fuel pump before I could drive it off the used car lot.

We pooled our resources for gas and toll fees and headed for New York. We arrived at Temple #7 about 7:30 p.m. and rushed upstairs. The Temple was on the third floor, and the elevator was too small and too slow, and we were young, still in our early and mid-twenties, so those three flights of stairs presented no problems.

We had to enter the Temple through what was called the "check room" where to my surprise we were all thoroughly searched before we entered the Temple where the F.O.I meeting would take place.

There were no chairs on the floor of this large loft room. The chairs were neatly stacked against the wall and at 8:00 p.m. the lieutenant barked out the order, "Fruit, fall in!"

Well, as you can imagine, I had no idea what he was talking about, so I just followed what I saw the majority of the brothers doing.

The East Coast Regional Captain's name was Joseph. He was a kind-of-short diminutive man about 5'7" tall. The Lieutenant called the Captain, and he addressed us for about 30 minutes on promptness, being on time, security, appearance —all the brothers dressed in suits, white shirts, and neckties or bow ties.

A group of brothers gathered in front of Temple #7's restaurant

When the Captain finished, he called for Brother Curtis 2X our drill instructor. He barked his orders, "Fruit, attention! Left face, right face, about face." At that time I stepped out of line. I could not follow. The brothers were walking all over my shoes.

There were over three hundred brothers at the F.O.I class meeting that night, and they seemed to be enjoying the drilling and calisthenics. Not I, because I had never done that before except in school, and my mind and body coordination were not clicking yet.

The Captain saw me standing against the wall watching the marching and told me to fall back into the ranks. I did. Soon I started clicking along with the brothers, a little.

About fifteen minutes before the F.O.I class was due to be dismissed, Minister Malcolm X came in and addressed the F.O.I. He told us how important it was to help the Honorable Elijah Muhammad build the Nation of Islam into a vital and visible organization by taking the message to the streets in pamphlets and word of mouth. Go to the poolrooms, the barbershops, the hair salons, the parks, and wherever you see people assembled, he said. Visit churches and social clubs Malcolm told us, but never nightclubs, bars, or dance halls.

After Malcolm X's talk, I was all pumped up, and ready to bring the whole city where I grew up to the Nation of Islam. Temple #7 had a restaurant on the ground level. We bought some sandwiches to go and started that long night journey back to Hartford, Connecticut, it was a long 120-mile drive, but we did not complain at all; we loved it.

The first business that every Temple opened, numbered or unnumbered, was a restaurant. It was a gathering place or waterhole for brothers and sisters to discuss Islam and make plans for Temple activities. It was also a place where non-Muslims would come, share a delicious pork-free meal and discuss current events with the brothers and sisters.

For three months we made that trip to New York every Monday night for F.O.I training and we were never late. The training taught security, discipline, 'general orders,' physical body searching, self-defense tactics, and the importance of cleanliness of body and soul.

"All F.O.I are to be clean at all times. Faces shaved, hair combed, suits cleaned and pressed, shoes shined. He must be quick thinking, fast moving, clean in and out, right down to the modern times. If you do not clean up, you are out of luck with us. And, all F.O.I must have some type of employment. No freeloaders or foot draggers."

"Laziness is idleness, and, an idle mind is the devil's workshop."

Enforcement of these rules was strict. In fact, no non-Muslim was allowed in the Temple unless properly dressed, and if any trace of alcohol or drugs was detected, during the physical body search, they could not enter.

Non-Muslim women's dresses had to be at least down to the knees to be allowed in Temple meetings, and the seating began on the 2nd row. The first row was reserved for Muslim sisters in their long garments to shield the non-Muslim's bare legs and undergarments from the brothers on the front post and the minister.

The F.O.I was considered the backbone of the Nation of Islam. They protected each other and with special emphasis were sworn to protect the sisters and all Temple property in view. He provides for his home and family. He fights, if necessary, and trains to fight. However, never is he the aggressor. He is ever on the alert. He sets an example by deeds not lip service. He is very clean both inside and outside, physically and mentally. And, he maintains respect for all people, treating them, as he, himself, would like to be treated.

After only three months of training, the Lieutenant of the Temple (we didn't have a Captain because we didn't have a numbered Temple) made me a squad leader. We only had enough brothers for one squad, and I was selected as leader.

The Lieutenant gave me a duplicate of all the keys to the Temple, and for one moment I felt very important, in fact, euphoric. Then I heard my assignment.

I was to be at the Temple at least one hour before the doors were scheduled to open. That meant two hours before the meeting starts. Sweep the floor. If necessary, mop, and then clean the bathroom. Clean the blackboard, and reset the 100 chairs. Arrange them perfectly. We were still renting the hall from the North-End Community Center and sharing it with the Moorish Americans, who met the night before.

By late 1956 we needed larger quarters because we had grown so much. We found a building on Albany Avenue. We renovated, moved in, and within three months we opened a restaurant right across the street. We were growing in numbers so fast that we expected to receive our number for the Temple, soon.

Every Temple had to ascribe to a process. It was about the numbers. Your Temple had to reach a certain number of registered believers before consideration for a number. It was hard work, delicate work, but it was all worth it.

In late 1956 Boston received its number, #11. Right behind Boston, Philadelphia received its number, #12. In early in 1957,

Springfield, Massachusetts received its number, #13, and in mid-1957 Hartford, Connecticut, received its number, #14.

At the 1957 Moslem Convention, the Honorable Elijah Muhammad had as his guest Mr. A. D. Gaither, Circulation Manager of one of the oldest African-American Newspapers in America, the Pittsburg Courier, and Mr. Ted Watson, the Courier's Chicago Editor, as well as the Courier's Advertising Representative and Photographer, Mr. Bozeman. They were there to present a plaque to the Honorable Elijah Muhammad, a "Pittsburg Courier Achievement Award."

In early 1956, the Honorable Elijah Muhammad had signed an agreement with the Pittsburg Courier to have the F.O.I sell their paper in every city where there was a Temple. Temples were in over 40 cities at that time.

Pittsburgh Courier - 1957

The compensation was that every salesperson would earn money from each sale, with compensation sent to the #2 Poor Treasury, and the Pittsburgh Courier would carry a weekly column, written by the Honorable Elijah Muhammad each week. The sales of the Courier soared. Our Temple used to sell over a thousand copies. I use to sell 100 copies.

The "Pittsburg Courier Achievement Award" was presented and read at the Convention in 1957 by Mr. A. D. Gaither. It read:

In The Name of Allah, The Beneficent, The Merciful

To: The Honorable Elijah Muhammad

In Recognition of Outstanding Achievement As Messenger

And Spiritual Leader Of Muhammad's Temples of Islam

Presented at

Annual Convention Chicago, Illinois

February 26, 1957

By the Pittsburg Courier Publishing Co.

Mr. Robert L. Vann, President

Now, we had leverage with the Courier. We asked for two things.

One, The Honorable Elijah Muhammad's article to post on the same page each week and two, an encased byline printed on the front of the paper with The Honorable Elijah Muhammad's name and the page his article appeared.

Both parties were pleased with the results.

We sold the Courier Newspaper until Minister Malcolm X founded the "Mr. Muhammad Speaks Newspaper" in late 1959-60, in Harlem, New York.

Next, Ebony Magazine, the African-American Bourgeoisie Society magazine came calling. They wanted the Honorable Elijah Muhammad's group to sell subscriptions to their magazine in exchange for farmland in the state of Michigan. We sold thousands of subscriptions to Ebony magazine and Johnson Publishing Company; they kept their promise and purchased fertile farmland for us in Michigan, totaling 1,000 acres.

Among the other materials that we use to sell was a small magazine that covered the Saviour's Day Conventions. The magazine, "The Moslem World and the U.S.A." only sold for $1.00 and was widely circulated by us.

Moslem World & The U.S.A. — April-May 1957

In the 1956 October, November, December Special Issue of Moslem World and the U.S.A, The Editor-Publisher, Mr. Abdul Basit Naeem writes:

"Moslem World & The U.S.A. is an independent publication. It is not the property of Mr. Elijah Muhammad or, for that matter, of anyone else other than its publisher. However, realizing that both Mr. Muhammad and his Moslem movement have become an inseparable part of the overall picture of Islamic affairs in America, we consider it our duty to print periodically, detailed reports of their progress.

As we see it, Mr. Muhammad's teaching offered through his Temples' (columns) (printed regularly in the Weekly "Pittsburgh Courier") have enabled more Americans to form acquaintance with Islam than the efforts of all other individuals seeking converts to Islam here put together. We are aware of the fact that Mr. Elijah Muhammad, as some Moslems have put it, "operates on racial lines." In other words, he considers and speaks of Islam as a "religion for black mankind." However, it is not difficult for us to comprehend the wisdom in such a practice on his part.

Mr. Muhammad believes that to preach Islam among "the whites" is to "waste one's time and effort" because he is convinced that they "just won't accept Islam and give it a place in their hearts." Besides, Mr. Muhammad believes that his convictions in this respect are definitely "divine" in nature and thus infallible. In our opinion, it is quite all right if only Black Americans ("the so-called Negroes") turn Moslem. Interested in the Mission and propagation of Islam as we are, we would rather see an all-black Moslem community in America than none at all.

Let's face it; a lot of people just wouldn't accept some of the basic principles of Islam, especially the Unity of Godhead, daily prayers, and abstention from intoxicants.

A few of our New York City friends recently asked us, in telephone conversation, whether or not we could "comment on Mr. Muhammad as an individual." What we told our friends over the telephone, we now record below in writing and in print. We believe that Mr. Muhammad is a very sincere leader of his people.

We believe he is not desirous of riches or fame. He is not worldly— he neither drinks nor smokes, nor does he eat but one meal a day. Moreover, by preaching what he does, he is constantly courting the wrath of his enemies. If Mr. Muhammad loved life, surely he would shun dangers!

Certain other friends of ours allege that Mr. Muhammad's Moslem teachings differ from those of Eastern Moslem. Mr. Muhammad readily concedes this, explaining that, "My people must be dealt with on a special basis because their background and circumstances are different from those prevailing elsewhere in the world. You cannot use the same medicine to treat an altogether different diseases," he says.

Here we might add that Mr. Muhammad doesn't think too much of some of the Eastern Moslems anyway, particularly those residing in this country where, he claims, "Their contact with a strange civilization has turned them into hypocrites of the worst type." The fact that Moslem grocers in Iowa, Ohio, California, and Michigan handle liquors and pork products and nearly all Moslem diplomats at the United Nations and in Washington, D.C, New York and San Francisco freely indulge in drinking greatly disturbs him. The behavior of many Moslem students in America doesn't impress him either.

A few of the Moslem groups in the United States have alleged, in letters to a prominent Moslem leader abroad, that Mr. Elijah Muhammad's followers 'aren't taught to perform their daily prayers.' Mr. Muhammad emphatically denies this, saying that, "The day is nearing when you will see them climbing to the top of minarets, proclaiming the Glory of Allah, and flocking to the mosques as good Moslems do in Saudi Arabia, Iraq, Morocco, and Pakistan." According to Mr. Muhammad, a mosque will be erected for Moslems wherever there is a Temple of Islam in America, the latter being a lecture hall or "place of instruction for those seeking the Truth—Islam."

Of all the Moslem leaders in this country, Mr. Muhammad is the only one who has shown any amount of concern for the education of Moslem children. The University of Islam in Chicago is a living proof of his desire to see to it that Moslem children are given an education that equals the best in Christian or public schools.

Mr. Muhammad also holds the unique distinction of being a "protector" of Moslem women. His teaching includes a number of strict regulations the women members of his Temples of Islam must abide by: full length, high neck, long sleeve dresses; no dancing or night-clubbing; segregation of sexes at Temple services. Mr.

Muhammad tells his male followers to respect their sisters-in-Islam in the same manner in which they would respect their blood sisters. It is no exaggeration to state that a Moslem follower of Mr. Elijah Muhammad would quickly lay down his life rather than see a sister molested or dishonored."

To others, and me, this article made it crystal clear that the Honorable Elijah Muhammad did not teach the rituals of religion. He only pointed out to his followers and others that he saw his work among the African-Americans as a messenger and social reformer to a people, lost and forgotten about by unconscionable American so-called whites, and he used those many titles as a means to attract.

According to this article, the Honorable Elijah Muhammad articulated the difference between a Mosque and a Temple. A Temple is a place where people are taught and encouraged to wake up, clean up and stand up. A sort of educational and wudu station, whereas a Mosque is only a place to pray.

In 1930 there was only one Qur'an translated into English by a knowledgeable Muslim Scholar in circulation, and that translation was by Maulana Muhammad Ali, who was from India. Mr. W. D. Fard introduced that one to the community.

CHAPTER 7:
Our "Proto-Islamic" Growth

Elijah Muhammad was born in 1897 as Elijah Poole. He went to school long enough to learn how to read and write, and he said his favorite reading book was the Bible. But he had to quit school to work and help his father support the family.

He knew absolutely nothing about Islam and Muslims until being introduced to this message at a Temple meeting in 1931 by Mr. W. D. Fard.

He accepted the message and became the top and the most progressive student of Mr. W. D. Fard. He was a student of the Bible and the most knowledgeable. The only knowledge he had of Islam was taught to him by Mr. W. D. Fard. To help him in his studies he (Mr. Fard) gave him the name of 104 books on history and Islam. The most important book the Honorable Elijah Muhammad said was "The Holy Qur'an," which was translated by Maulana Muhammad Ali.

He became Mr. W. D. Fard's most promising student minister, soon to be called the Supreme Minister. Mr. W. D. Fard wrote a series of lessons that he taught his students. None of the lessons Mr. W. D. Fard left was on religion. In English Lesson #C-1 he wrote that we were Muslims before we were brought to America and that we are Muslim now.

The Lesson also read in part:

"Know yourself and be yourself. Who is myself? Myself is a righteous Muslim. Are there any Muslims other than righteous? I beg your pardon, I have never heard of one."

The Honorable Elijah Muhammad knew that he was not the one to teach the rituals of religion. His mission was to keep his people, from drowning in the fire of sin, and clean them up, preparing them for the religion of Islam. In order to do that he needed help. So in 1947, the Honorable Elijah Muhammad hired a Palestinian refugee, Professor Jameel Diab to teach Qur'anic Arabic in his University of Islam School in Chicago. He called his school "University" because they were teaching universal knowledge there, he said.

What became of those students after being introduced to Qur'anic Arabic under Professor Jameel Diab? One—Akbar Muhammad, is a Professor at a leading US University and another (Darnell Karim) is an Imam who teaches Qur'anic Arabic classes in many areas of America. Another traveled the world of Muslims, studying and observing Islam in practice and eventually succeeded his father as leader, Imam W. Deen Mohammed — who changed the communities name and direction and continued the reformation and evolutionary transition to Universal Islamic thought and practice. They all made significant contributions in different cities, under trying circumstances in America, introducing Islam to the African-American people.

Eventually appointed to the position of first Lieutenant and acting Captain of Temple #14, in 1959 I became Assistant

Minister. That position gave me the time and opportunity to travel to other cities in Connecticut, where I began to introduce people to the message of the Nation of Islam.

I took with me copies of the three newspapers we were selling at that time: the Pittsburg Courier, New York Amsterdam News, and the Los Angeles Herald-Dispatch. My intention was to make friends and identify people that were sympathetic to our cause. Many friends and sympathetic people began to look forward to my coming as I traveled from barbershops to hair and beauty salons.

More brothers began to travel with me, and soon we were meeting in the living room of a believing Muslim family—Brother Harold and Sister Martha, who like me, came from The Moorish American community.

The first time I met Minister Wallace D. Muhammad (Imam W. Deen Mohammed) was in 1959. He was on a speaking tour that started in Boston, Massachusetts and continued to Springfield, MA; Hartford, CT; Harlem, NY; and finally to Philadelphia, PA where he was to become their new minister. Accompanying him on his speaking tour was Minister Malcolm X, Supreme Captain Raymond Sharrieff, and the National M.G.T Captain Ethel Sharrief.

Minister Malcolm X opened the meeting in each Temple and introduced Minister Wallace D., the son of the Honorable Elijah Muhammad. As an F.O.I Captain, I accompanied the group with a few selected brothers who were at the top of the security class in self-defense, to all the cities where the group went.

Minister Wallace, in his talks, introduced Arabic script to his audience as he explained Qur'anic Chapters, Al-Faatihah and Al-

Ikhlas. Temple #14 in Hartford was the last stop on Minister Wallace Muhammad's tour before Temple #7 in Harlem.

East Coast regional Captain Joseph sent a security group from New York to take charge of the security and escort the group to New York.

Minister Malcolm X, the Honorable Elijah Muhammad's National Representative, really didn't begin to be a national public figure until a household invasion by the New York City police critically injured a member of the Harlem Temple.

The brother was taken to the police station and beaten in the head and knees by the police and not given any medical attention until Minister Malcolm and Captain Joseph went there to protest. The brother's head wound was severe. The news media followed.

With the brother finally getting released for medical attention, the call went out to every Temple on the East Coast. Muslims and non-Muslims converged upon Harlem Hospital by the thousands standing at attention, not saying a word, but keeping vigil and praying for the brother's recovery.

I led a squad of brothers who were assigned to cover 125th Street and Lenox Avenue, directing all passersby to Harlem Hospital. Then, I joined the hundreds of brothers from as far away as Massachusetts and Washington, DC at the Harlem hospital, standing in ranks, at attention and not moving or speaking, but waiting for instructions from Captain Joseph.

Minister Malcolm X was inside the hospital, Captain Joseph was standing at the top of the stairs leading into the hospital, and we were waiting in front of the hospital, blocking all walking and automobile traffic, in silence, waiting on the news of the condition of the brother.

After an extended length of time, Malcolm X came out of the hospital, whispered something to Captain Joseph, Captain Joseph called the lieutenant, and the word was: "the brother is recovering from his operation." The Lieutenant barked, "Attention, dismiss." We were dismissed and told to re-assemble at Temple #7.

Quicker than you can say the word, we were gone. A police captain is reported to have said about Minister Malcolm X, "No man should have that much power!"

Because we stood up, the fear of us in some African-Americans and European-Americans turned to admiration.

The New York Amsterdam News leading article was: "God's Angry Men, with whom are they angry and why"? If that brother had died, only God knows what would have happened that night. But it would not have been pretty.

The M.G.T and G.C.C (Muslim Girl Training and General Civilization Class) were equally as important to the progress of the Lost-Found Members of the Nation of Islam as the F.O.I (Fruit of Islam). They had their class and Captain and Lieutenants.

The sisters, as a group, had drill instructors who also led them in exercises and self-defense. The cap of the uniforms they wore was designed to protect them from a head injury if the police ever unlawfully attacked our places of worship. Maintenance of the home, children, and Temple property were vital concerns to them, and they studied in the M.G.T Class how to secure them.

We can't overlook the efforts of the Black women in the history of the African-American struggle from slavery to Emancipation to freedom to citizenship rights.

We must remember the courage and commitment of these women, such as Harriet Tubman, Sojourner Truth, Daisy Bates, Rosa Parks, as well as some outstanding European-American women who stood tall in the face of much public adversity. Like Mrs. Eleanor Roosevelt, and the Quaker women who were abolitionists and helpers of Sojourner Truth, and others who secured safe-houses for escaping slaves who found refuge in the North and Canada through a system called the Underground Railroad.

As amazing and courageous as these women were, none stood taller in our community than Sister Clara Muhammad, wife of the Honorable Elijah Muhammad, builder of the Nation of Islam.

It was Sister Clara Muhammad who attended the meetings of Mr. W. D. Fard in Detroit, first. And, it was Sister Clara Muhammad who convinced her husband, Elijah, to come and hear this man. It was Sister Clara Muhammad who raised their eight children and held the community together, after Mr. W. D. Fard's departure in 1934, when the hypocrites rose up and attempted to kill her husband, driving him out of Chicago where for the next eight years he could only visit his family in secret or at night. After the hypocrite's threat was over, the Government in 1942 arrested her husband charging him with failure to register for the military draft and sent him to prison until the war was over.

During the Honorable Elijah Muhammad's incarceration, it was Sister Clara Muhammad who kept him informed and abreast on family matters and the condition and progress of the community. While serving his time in prison, The Honorable

Elijah Muhammad befriended a prison guard who supplied him with a blackboard, chalk, and some paint.

He drew a blackboard in prison, precisely like the one Mr. W. D. Fard had drawn in Detroit and subsequently used in all Temple meetings, to teach the inmates what Mr. W. D. Fard had taught him and others.

It was here that the Muslim prison ministry saw its beginning. The Honorable Elijah Muhammad taught the same thing in prison that he taught in the Temples outside of prison. He did not change a thing. The only Muslims that went to prison in those days were conscientious objections, not criminal activities.

As Assistant Minister at Temple #14 in Hartford, I had progressed through the ranks along with others. Much responsibility came with being active community members. We had to learn the duties of each Temple position we were assigned and the position directly above us. Our preparation was necessary for any eventuality.

We worked our day or night jobs, and we took care of our families; we gave charity, and we performed our duties either in the Temple teaching others or out in the field sharing the message with non-Muslims — a method we called "fishing and propagation." "Fishing" is what we called inviting people to Temple meetings.

The minister used to encourage the members to bring new people to Temple meeting. Public meetings took place three times per week: Wednesday night and Friday night at 8:00 p.m., and Sunday at 2:00 p.m.

The minister of the Temple emphasized the importance of going beyond our comfort zone of relatives, friends, acquaintances, and cast our net. The bait was in the language. The message was self-pride, self-awareness, self-esteem, self-value, self-respect, and the unity of self to do for self and sustain what we have by supporting one another.

We had a dress code: "The first impression is the lasting impression." Therefore, our clothing had to be similar to the clothing of the people we were trying to attract with our message, but better. Our physical appearance was of great importance to our mission. Our appearance had to be impressive, not gaudy or rich looking, but spic and span.

To invite someone to something different from what they have, and have them accept to come and listen, your appearance, your message, and your language had to be appealing. When a person goes fishing for the water fish, he baits the hook with what the fish like, not what he likes.

The idea for the term "fishing" came from the Bible:

"And Jesus, walking by the Sea of Galilee, saw two brethren, Simon [called Peter], and Andrew his brother, casting a net into the sea, for they were fishers." — St. Matthew 4:18 *"And he saith unto them, follow me, and I will make you fishers of men."* — St Matthew 4:19

We traveled in twos, when possible, as a partner and witness, and brought with us our best behavior and conduct. Always say thank you, yes ma'am and yes sir, no ma'am, and no sir. We were encouraged and supported by our home Temple to take the message into cities and towns with sizable African-American populations, where no one was currently teaching and spreading the word.

As new and young members of the Nation of Islam, we were eager to learn. One of the instructions of the Nation was, "Make all men and boys join the F.O.I class and train them fast. Make them brave warriors willing to give their life at any time for the cause of Islam." The cause of Islam was to achieve freedom, justice, and equality by the method that God had made available to us, not "by any means necessary," but by peaceful means.

Any means necessary is un-Islamic. Justice, we were taught, was nearer to righteousness. Captain Joseph X of Temple #7, of Harlem, New York City, instilled within us, in the F.O.I Class, the Honorable Elijah Muhammad statement that peace was the way of the righteous.

We learned that message thoroughly, and took the courage to leave the established Temple and follow the example of generations before us, and try and duplicate their heroic efforts.

That decision earned us the title of Field Minister.

In a letter to the ministry class dated December 1934, the Honorable Elijah Muhammad wrote:

> "Go, and make many ministers and send them in all of the cities. Let us not rely on the already converted ones of another minister's, but concentrate on the ability of ourselves as to how many can we bring to the fold of Islam through our faith and individual efforts."

We were busy every day, seven days a week without fail. We were not driven; we drove ourselves by the message that, "It was the duty of the civilized to teach the uncivilized."

The message to all of the men who belonged to Islam in North American was: "Hurry, Hurry, Hurry! Lose no more time.

Have no quarreling among the believers; the law settles all arguments. Big fields await the wide-awake man to work out in. So, get busy and raise the dead by the thousands".

The Honorable Elijah Muhammad wrote five books explaining his message and reformation of the African-American descendants of slaves:

- Message to the Blackman;
- Our Savior Has Arrived
- Fall of America
- How to Eat to Live (part 1 and 2)

The Nation of Islam published these books, and members sold them to further the propagation and its efforts.

In 1961, at the age of 30, I moved from Hartford to New Haven, CT to concentrate on building a Temple. Married, with a nine-year-old son, I found work in dry cleaners. My experience managing that business for my oldest brother provided knowledge of every aspect of that business. He had also hired an experienced man who taught me everything he knew: from pick-up to delivery to running a cleaning unit, spotting, and pressing everything from rough pieces to silks to pleats. Plus, I was dependable.

An experienced person always could find work in the dry cleaning business, and I preferred it because my time was my own. There was no clock to punch and wages paid according to the number of clothes finished. Moreover, I could leave whenever necessary. That provided more time to study, execute Temple duties, and propagate our message.

My profession was photography. I went to school for that. However, in the late 40's and 50's, newspapers and magazines hired very few African-Americans. It was a dead profession for me, so I joined my brother in the dry cleaning business. He was hurt when I left, but it was time to move on. I couldn't see myself in a 9 to 5 job when there were so many of our people out there falling through the cracks of society.

Our mother, my younger brother Charles Lester (Abdul Majid), and I were still living in the eighteen-room, three-story, three family house we owned, and well on our way to middle-class living when I made my decision to move. I left the safe comfort of home ownership and family surroundings to establish a Temple in New Haven, Connecticut.

After securing a job and an apartment, I moved my wife and son to New Haven. Our mother had been an activist during the Marcus Garvey and Noble Drew Ali era and supported and encouraged our decision.

Not very many people in New Haven knew about what we represented or us. Our main disadvantage for was name recognition. The name that identified us in those days was Black Muslims. The author of the popular book Black Muslims in America, Dr. C. Eric Lincoln, gave this name to us in the early 1960s. He was a noted sociologist of great distinction, who also referred to us as a Proto-Islamic Group, a startling observation by a Christian scholar who was wise enough to see that we, as a community, were evolving into the genuine universal Muslim community.

The people gradually began to connect us with this name 'Black Muslims,' but it was not a name we promoted. We promoted the idea that we were Muslims, but not by the name, 'Black Muslims', which was extensively used by so-called white people and immigrant Muslims. Their usage had a negative connotation to it.

From the message of the Nation of Islam, we learned to train the new converts fast. We were asked to encourage all that came to do all he or she could for the cause of Islam.

Fortunately, for us, in 1960, Minister Malcolm X founded a newspaper and named it "Mr. Muhammad Speaks." In the same year, the editorial staff of the paper moved to Chicago, and changed the name to "Muhammad Speaks."

Instead of "Muhammad Speaks" just being a local New York paper, by moving to Chicago, it instantly became our national paper. There was a new emphasis placed on us to take this paper to the streets because it provided our first opportunity to carry news from America and from around the Muslim world while educating the American public.

"Muhammad Speaks" newspaper aided us in spreading the idea that Islam was not a local religion believed by dark-skinned people only, but a universal religion with Muslim believers all over the world in countries such as Indonesia, Arabia, Pakistan, India, Europe, Africa, China, Malaysia, America, Turkey, South America, and others.

In the beginning, our Temple in New Haven ordered one thousand "Muhammad Speaks" newspapers, with one week to sell them. We set our quota at 300 per man and had to make our increase gradually. Remember, all of us worked eight-hour jobs. We had families and homes to maintain plus our charity for maintenance and upkeep of our Temples. It was not easy. We had many opportunities to turn back, but we did not. Our dedication was to an idea. So, after work, we sold papers in the neighborhoods where we lived. We were committed. No one committed us. We committed ourselves. No one obligated us. We obligated ourselves. All who came did not stay. Some dropped out. However, others who were even more committed to an idea and a bright future, rather than immediate gratification soon replaced them.

We sold "Muhammad Speaks" newspaper all over Southern Connecticut cities: New Haven, Bridgeport, Greenwich, Waterbury, Stanford, Norwalk, New London, Milford and at the hangouts of Yale students, social clubs. We saturated the area. We even brought our paper to the Federal Prison in Danbury, Connecticut.

In the meantime in 1962, Minister Malcolm X made four appearances at Yale University. He had two debates with Louis Lomax, the reporter who fronted for Mike Wallace as an interviewer of Minister Malcolm X and the Honorable Elijah

Muhammad for a CBS Special in the 1960s, "The Hate that Hate Produced," and he came one other time as the keynote speaker for a Yale student-sponsored event. Moreover, each time he spoke to a standing room only crowd. All of his Yale appearances helped us to increase our Temple membership in New Haven.

The last time Minister Malcolm X spoke in New Haven was in June 1963, when he honored my invitation to speak at a public event in a local middle school auditorium. The publicity from Minister Malcolm X's visit worried many local preachers. To try and minimize our effectiveness, especially among people our age, some of the preachers who felt threatened by our progress ventured to speak out against us.

One local Christian Minister who's church was next door to our Temple, on Dixwell Avenue, when asked during an interview with the New Haven Register Newspaper, said, *"Oh, they are a fly by night group. They won't be around long."*

Well, we are still here, so what poor insight he had.

We soon established ourselves as a viable part of the African-American community in Southern Connecticut and made such an impression that the Mayor and Police Chief would consult with us.

We opened three businesses: a restaurant, bakery, and a Muslim literature bookstore. All of them did quite well.

We made the best Philly steaks in New Haven and the best bean pies in Connecticut. We started out by buying our pies from the Muslim bakery in Long Island, New York. Our volume was significant, but our profit was small, so we started baking them ourselves. We sold the small pies, called "teenie beanie," to the supermarkets in New Haven and Waterbury. A sister would make the crust the night before, and after the Fajr (morning) prayer, I would come and prepare the mix and bake the pies, then, go to work. Our salesman, Brother Marion would come in after me, wrap the pies in plastic, and deliver them to the markets.

When I came home in the evening, I would work the bookstore, while other brothers and sisters handled the restaurant.

From the proceeds of our three businesses, we opened a full-time University of Islam School, bought two station wagons to transport our school-age children from as far away as Stamford (40 miles away), and provided them with lunch.

In the summer of 1965, the Honorable Elijah Muhammad called a National Laborers' meeting. He said in part: *"If you received this letter, you are invited to this meeting in Chicago, Temple #2. Don't mention this letter to anyone".*

I received a letter, and the only people that were allowed to attend this meeting had received a letter. The Honorable Elijah Muhammad spoke for a little over an hour. No one could take notes. Concentrating on what he had to say required strict attention by all in attendance.

After his talk, he went down the list of all in attendance. The laborers that he did not know, he asked to stand when he called their name.

One by one, brothers stood up and introduced themselves. He, finally, came upon my name and said, *"Abdel Krim El, would you please stand up?"* I stood up, and he said, *"Brother Minister, we don't take names for ourselves. Our Saviour said when he returns he will give all of us names".*

I explained to the Honorable Elijah Muhammad my family's history with the Marcus Garvey Movement and my uncle Mossa's fondness of the Moroccan Freedom Fighter, Abdel Krim.

The Honorable Elijah Muhammad told me to discontinue the use of the "El" because it only meant "THE" and that my Muslim name was sufficient. Then he said, now, these are his words; I remember them exactly.

"*Abdel Krim is a corruption of a bigger name.*" He said, "*The bigger name is pronounced Abdul Karriem.*"

Then, he said, "*I only desire for my followers the best. Abdel should be pronounced A-b-d-u-l.*" He spelled it and asked me to repeat it. I did, and he said, "Good."

"Krim," he said, "should be pronounced Karriem." Then, he spelled it: "K-a-r-r–i-e-m" and asked me to repeat the spelling.

I did, and he said, "You are very smart."

Then he said, "To your new acquaintances, introduce yourself as Abdul Karriem."

Coming back from that meeting with the Honorable Elijah Muhammad gave all the top laborers, ministers, captains, and secretaries a new spirit to do even more for the cause of Islam.

All laborers received a list of materials recommended to study, to prepare ourselves for the task ahead better. The list included lessons and books. Two books mentioned were on the Life of Prophet Muhammad (Peace and Blessings of Allah be upon him), and not easy to find in just any public library. I used to go to Yale University library in New Haven to read them. They were rare books that could not be checked out. So I used to take a pad with me to write notes.

Aids to help a speaker study to teach on the Honorable Elijah Muhammad and the religion of Islam were sent to us by the National Secretary in Chicago. The recommended list for reading and continued study materials were:

- Student Enrollment
- Lost Found Moslem Lesson #1
- Actual Fact
- Lost Found Moslem Lesson #2
- Problem Book (34 Problems)
- English Lesson #C-1
- Message to the Blackman by Elijah Muhammad
- The Holy Qur'an, Translation by Maulana Muhammad Ali
- Holy Bible, King James Version
- A Manual of Hadith
- The Life of Mohammad by Sir William Muir, K.C.S.I, Edited by T. H. Weir, B. D., M. R .A. S
- Life of Mohamet by Washington Irving
- The Religion of Islam: A Comprehensive Discussion of Its Sources, Principles and Practices by Maulana Muhammad Ali
- A Good Dictionary
- Roget's Thesaurus in dictionary form
- Cruden's Complete Concordance of The Old and New Testaments by Alexander Cruden, Edited by A. D Adams, C. H Irwin, S. A Waters
- Hammond-Dell World Atlas
- Biblical Names and Their Arabic Equivalents

Minister Louis X, with increased duties as Minister of Temple #7-C in Long Island, New York, could no longer service Bridgeport, Connecticut which was eighty miles away. So, he asked me to accept responsibility for its growth.

My younger brother Abdul Majid had finished his tour of duty in the United States Air Force and was a member of the

Temple in Hartford. After rising through the ranks as I did years before him and becoming a Captain of the F.O.I, he eventually resigned that position and joined us in New Haven.

With the additional responsibilities of the Temple in Bridgeport, we combined our strength and increased our presence in every city selling Muhammad Speaks and inviting people to our Temple meetings. Saturdays and Sundays were our most impactful days in our propagation efforts.

While the young men were busy selling their papers, the young women were busy preparing dinners that they would sell to customers in Beauty and Hair Salons to raise money for Temple maintenance and up-keep.

These scores of young men and women were committed to an idea and worked together like a well-oiled machine to make their contributions to a growing and vibrant African-American community. Moreover, these efforts were being duplicated in every city across America with a substantial population of African-Americans.

We were all young men and women with family obligations, but we were also on a mission. None of us was over thirty-five. We believed that if we could conceive what we wanted to establish and work hard at it, we could bring it into reality and with a pioneering spirit and unified effort we could achieve success. Thanks to Allah, we did.

We traveled in groups of two's and four's as a means of security, but we never had any confrontation with anyone. The people were mostly friendly, even if they did not buy a paper or accept our message. Our growth was phenomenal. We believed in friendly competition, always trying to out-do one another in everything: selling papers, charity, and physical exercise, keeping our Temple clean of filth at all time, and 'fishing' or bringing in new people to the Temple on meeting nights.

During that year, our Temple had registered enough Muslims to apply for a number. In those days any Temple that reached a sufficient number of registered believers (25) attending Temple meetings at least once a week was qualified for a number.

When I became a registered believer in 1956, there were only ten numbered Temples. When we applied for our numbers for New Haven and Bridgeport nine years later, there were 39 numbered Temples. We received our answer from the Honorable Elijah Muhammad's office in 1965. Our work had paid off. New Haven became Temple #40, and Bridgeport became Temple #41. We received these two numbers for these two cities in the same letter.

With the designation of these numbers, we became officially classified as Minister and Captain. I visited with the Honorable Elijah Muhammad on a one on one basis often after that, discussing our progress in Temple growth, National Business Plans, and infractions involving the Restricted Laws of Islam.

CHAPTER 8:
The City of Angels

The Honorable Elijah Muhammad started meeting with all the Temple ministers once a month. He began to distrust the mail, thereby requesting that the ministers bring the monthly reports of our Temple activities to Chicago each month. The East Coast Ministers would meet at his house over dinner on the first day of the month, and the West Coast Ministers would meet on the second day.

In late October 1971, after a dinner meeting in his home, the Honorable Elijah Muhammad reached into his suit jacket pocket and pulled out a slip of paper with ten items on it. He said he wanted us to help him find qualified people to fill needed positions in some of our larger Temples.

The first item on the list was Los Angeles, Temple #27. He said he needed a minister for Los Angeles. There was quiet in the room. No one said anything. So, I said, and I do not know why I said it, "I'll go."

He swiveled around in his chair and looked. I was not sitting at the long conference table. I was sitting at a smaller table to his right, maybe three feet away, but parallel to him.

He said, "Brother Minister, you already have two Temples."

I said, "I have two capable assistants that can handle each Temple."

He said, "Well, All right," then as an afterthought, he said, "how large is your family?"

I responded, "I have a wife and son."

He said, "Okay, we have our minister for Los Angeles."

Then he quoted a Bible verse, Isaiah 6:8:

"When the Lord said, Whom shall I send, and who will go for us? Then, said (Isaiah), Here I am; send me".

The Honorable Elijah Muhammad finished the discussion on Los Angeles, asking me to come back to the house at 10:00 a.m. the next day for instructions.

Arriving ahead of time that following morning, I receive special instructions to investigate a situation in Los Angeles and report back to him in ten days.

He provided one thousand dollars for transportation and hotel expenses and sent me to the west coast.

After arriving in Los Angeles for this investigative visit, the first person I saw at the airline gate was Second Lieutenant Bartha (Naim Shah), and the next person was First Captain Edward (Ali Rashid).

Ten days later, I returned and reported my assessment to the Honorable Elijah Muhammad, who was satisfied with the written report.

Then, he asked if I had a copy of the Restricted Laws of Islam. I said yes.

"Put the Restricted Law in your pocket," he said, "and make that your first subject of Friday night." In his parting words, he said, "Go back to Connecticut; close out your affairs; take your wife and son and any personal things you need, and be back in Los Angeles by Friday."

Regional F.O.I Captain Joseph of Temple #7 in Harlem, New York, and his wife, Sylvia, invited us to a farewell dinner before my wife and I left for Los Angeles to assume my post as the Honorable Elijah Muhammad's representative and the West Coast Regional Minister. He also invited Regional Captain Sister Clotel and her husband, William to join us. My wife, Na'imah, was also an M.G.T Captain. She was the only minister's wife that the Honorable Elijah Muhammad, officially allowed to be a Captain. She was invited to his house along with Sister Captain Clotel for a weekend visit with him and his wife, Sister Clara, after which he authorized her appointment.

During our dinner in New York City, Captain Joseph told us at the table that when the Honorable Elijah Muhammad appointed me to the position as Minister at Los Angeles Temple #27, Captain Elijah Muhammad Jr. called him and instructed him to investigate me. Captain Joseph was laughing as he made the comments. He said his response to him was, "What? I trained him. I've worked with him for fifteen years. I've watched him grow and develop in this community. He has always been loyal and productive."

Some of the best advice that I have ever been fortunate to receive and benefit from came from Captain Joseph. At the end of the evening, he said, "Listen, when you go to Los Angeles don't mention to the body of Muslims the faults of the three previous Ministers that caused their dismissal. There are people there that love them, and you will only turn them against you. Remember, they are not your converts. You go to work, encourage the members to bring new people to the meeting and gradually you will win them over. If you are asked about the previous ministers, just tell them that the Honorable Elijah Muhammad had adjudicated their affairs and it is now settled." To this day, I have not discussed anyone's shortcomings because we all have them. Only Allah is Perfect.

A few days later, November 5, 1971, we left for Los Angeles, without our son Kenneth, who was a student at Antioch College in Yellow Springs Ohio. We arrived in Los Angeles on United Airlines. Meeting my wife and me at the airport were Captain Edward (Ali Rashid) and Brother Dennis (Khalil Karim), the President of Magnificent Brothers Hair Products. They took us to the Ambassador Hotel on Wilshire. It was sad to say, but that classic hotel that used to look so elegant on Hollywood television shows had seen its better days. It still had its beautiful landscaping, but the inside decor was no longer fashionable.

Three ministers of Temple #27 served before me; Minister John Shabazz, Minister Herman Rasul, and Minister Bashir Muhammad. The Honorable Elijah Muhammad removed them from their position for some reason, and I never brought it up in my talks. For those wanting to know, the answer was, "Their situation has been resolved by the Honorable Elijah Muhammad, and we are concentrating on what happens from this present time. This is day one for me and we will start together from here and move forward". As instructed, my first talk was about the Restricted Laws of Islam.

Brother Lieutenant Willie Wali Muhammad found this house on Don Miguel that was for lease. He and several brothers fixed it up, and my wife and I moved in.

Muhammad's Temple #27's address was 5606 South Broadway. They had bought the two-story building sometime in the late 1950s, and the building accommodated the University of Islam School upstairs and the Temple auditorium downstairs.

The first time I visited Temple #27 was in 1960 when the Honorable Elijah Muhammad was in Los Angeles to make a public address at the old Olympic Boxing Arena. I flew in with a group of brothers from Boston, and we stayed at the Olympian Hotel on Olympic Boulevard.

All the ministers and brothers and sisters who could afford it came to Los Angeles from the East Coast to hear and support the Honorable Elijah Muhammad. Included were Minister Malcolm X from Temple #7, Harlem, New York; Minister Isaiah from Temple #6, Baltimore; Minister Jeremiah from Philadelphia; Minister Lucious Bey from Miami; Minister Louis from Boston, and Minister Malcolm X's; two brothers from Detroit, Wilfred, and Philbert (both were ministers).

On Saturday, before the Honorable Elijah Muhammad's talk on Sunday, Minister Philbert, Minister Wilfred and I drove to Tijuana, Mexico, and later we visited Disneyland.

People packed the Olympic Arena that day. No so-called whites were allowed in. My duty was to take charge of the arena entrance and keep the peace. There were so-called white people across the street demonstrating with large signs saying, "This is America; they won't let us in." "They teach hate." However, things were peaceful.

The Muslim brothers in Los Angeles had a rich history of progress and activism; they were selling three different newspapers that carried our message: Muhammad Speaks, Los Angeles Herald-Dispatch, and a smaller paper originating in Long Beach written for by Minister Randolph (Wazir).

The sixties were very turbulent for Muslims in Los Angeles, however. Twice the Los Angeles Police department broke into the Temple. When the unarmed brothers resisted, one brother, who was the secretary was shot dead. Several others were also wounded, and many more arrested. During the 1965 riot, the Los Angeles Sentinel Newspaper headlines read 'The Police Attack the Muslims.'

However, that did not stop anything; unprovoked force never does. An unintended consequence was the galvanizing of non-Muslim intellectuals and politicians on behalf of the Muslims. These non-Muslim supporters may not have accepted our message, but they knew we were peaceful because we lived in the same community as they and for the most part prevented violence. Moreover, they admired people who would stand up and fight for their rights, freedom of speech, freedom of religion and public assembly.

The attack on our Temple was another attempt to put fear in us, but it failed. Our Temple membership grew even faster. They tried to stop us from selling our religious paper in our community to our people on public streets, and that did not work.

With water hoses blowing peaceful people's clothing off in the South, trained dogs attacking women, children, men (both black and white), and Northern policeman knocking down doors of peaceful people's houses of worship under false pretenses of seeing guns and finding none—finally, the slow, lumbering, Federal Government stepped in to restore some signs of civil civilization.

Things were a little more peaceful when I arrived in Los Angeles in October 1971 as we set out to establish the programs of The Honorable Elijah Muhammad in Los Angeles.

Our Programs:

1. Increase our efforts in propagation:
    - Muhammad Speaks (the number one tool)
    - Establish a live weekly TV program

2. Invite more people to the Temple meetings
    - Clean them up of gambling, games of chance, drinking alcohol, smoking, extramarital affairs, drugs (heroin, cocaine, reefers)

3. Start new businesses
    - Create jobs

These programs and others were a mandate for us.

The first business established by Temple #27 under my leadership was a Dry Cleaners. Believers in the Temple already had restaurants, grocery stores, shoe stores, fast food, and they were doing quite well. So, we always reminded people to patronize them.

Within a year we outgrew the facilities on Broadway. We started a fundraising drive to raise money to buy something more spacious, something with off street parking.

The Old Elks Club building on Central Avenue was for sale. One of our real estate brokers handled the negotiations and paperwork, and we bought the building. We paid $180,000 with a $50,000 down payment, and a payoff in 10 years. We took possession of the building May 30, 1973.

We completely renovated the Elks building. It took us only 30 days to do it, and we were ready for our first meeting.

Old Elks Club Building, 1973

Elk's building after renovation — Masjid Felix Bilal

We had six storefronts in the Elks building, and we opened businesses in all of them.

In 1983, we "burnt the mortgage note."

The Nation of Islam under The Honorable Elijah Muhammad's leadership, bought an old World War II B-24 airplane that flew our papers to Los Angeles, stopping at several locations on the route here in 1972.

The Temples in Southern California were selling over 75,000 papers, weekly. More and more people were responding to our message. There were Temples in Bakersfield, Pasadena, Compton, Long Beach, Pomona, Riverside, San Bernardino, Pacoima, and three new Temples in Los Angeles: Watts, Westside, Central Avenue, as well as the original Temple on Broadway.

San Diego Temple, the oldest on the West Coast, was designated Muhammad's Temple #8 a long time before Los Angeles received the designation of Temple #27.

Our big business boost came in 1972 when the Honorable Elijah Muhammad established a Muhammad's Import Company and began importing clothes, shoes, and kitchenware from Japan and South Korea. We were also importing whiting fish or hake fish from Japan. Because of our volume of sales and the fishing company in Japan's refusal to negotiate a lower price, the Honorable Elijah Muhammad sent his National Secretary, Abass Rassoull and his Import C.E.O, Nadar Ali, to other countries to negotiate for products at reasonable costs.

In 1973, National Secretary, Abass Rassoull and Muhammad's Import C.E.O, Nadar Ali, were sent to Peru. There they negotiated a contract with the Peruvian Government to ship to us 12,000 metric tons (2,645,520 pounds) of Whiting H&G (headed and gutted) fish a year for three years.

Four ships sailed into Los Angeles Harbor in 1973 and 1974 with one ship, a Panamanian flag ship flying our flag —the Sun, Crescent Moon and Star and carrying a total of over 550,000 pounds of our fish.

Union crews unloaded three ships at the docks, with the last ship unloaded by the F.O.I and stored in our 200,000 lb. freezer on South Vermont. We were able to supply every Temple on the West Coast with freshly frozen fish.

Peruvian and National of Islam Officials, in Peru
Second to left, Nadar Ali, fifth from left Abass Rassoull

A.K. Hasan (left) and Charles 7X at the LA Harbor

Because of the revenue generated from the fish sales, Temple #27 bought seven panel-refrigerated trucks for the fish crew's door-to-door sales, a tractor & trailer, and a fourteen-foot freezer truck for deliveries.

We opened six fish and poultry markets with modern showcases, seven take-out fast food fish and chicken restaurants, a 40,000 sq. ft. Supermarket (formerly Boys Market), a smaller one-stop grocery shop market on Jefferson Blvd., a Union Gasoline station, one bakery outlet, a wholesale warehouse and huge rotisserie bakery that supplied all our pies, bread, beans and french fries for our stores.

Refrigerated Truck (far left) - Door to Door Sales Vans on right

We had 23 businesses in total, employing well over 300 people, and that was just in Los Angeles. All the Temples were doing practically the same things.

We had a secretarial staff, an accounting staff, and a group of dedicated and committed F.O.I & M.G.T that were second to none.

CHAPTER 9:
Like All Living Creatures of G-d

At the arrival of 1974, the progress of Muhammad Temples of Islam was unprecedented. The laborers in every Temple in every section of the country were making enormous strides, and the men and women were looking forward to the annual Saviour's Day Convention in Chicago, not knowing that February 1974 would be The Honorable Elijah Muhammad's last Savior's Day Convention.

Though not in the best of health, Sister Captain Mamie Hudaa and I had the distinct pleasure of having dinner with the Honorable Elijah Muhammad and some of the other laborers at his new home that he called his 'kingdom,' the evening before the Saviour's Day Convention.

His Saviour's Day Speech was the next day at a packed National Guard Armory on Cottage Grove Avenue. It was on a Sunday and a frigid day in Chicago. Nevertheless, thousands were in line waiting for the doors to open. As the Honorable Elijah Muhammad walked in, escorted by his security, it was to a standing ovation. The Assistant Minister of Temple #2, Yusuf Shah, introduced him. His remarks that day reverberated through the audience in quiet anticipation to the thought-provoking message of a sage, talking to his family.

Excerpts from the Honorable Elijah Muhammad's Last Saviour's Day Convention Public Address February 1974:

"As-Salaam Alaikum, MY BELOVED BROTHERS AND SISTERS, we have here a very beautiful day from Allah. We are people that do not think we are big "I"s; we think that we are little "I"s and not big "I"s.

"We are greatly blessed by Allah, and by you visiting us that we cannot help but to be happy and proud of your presence.

"We want you to know that you have seen the setting of the sun, but that sun is rising again. It set but she is rising again, bringing us a new day, from the looks of your numbers here today it seems as if you are waking up.

"I remember the last time that I was out at the airport; they let me and my followers get on (the plane) first. Now, remember their flag is still flying over America; honor and respect the man, because he still has this land.

"There is much that can be interchanged between them and us in that way of respect. We don't have to get up to try and take from them just because you have learned yourself, and now you have learned them. Just remember that they show you respect after you have learned yourself, show them respect too, because when you didn't know yourself you didn't respect self or anyone else. We were a disgrace to ourselves and them. But now we respect ourselves and we respect them. Praise be to Allah.

"WE DON'T GO OUT and disrespect the owners of this land as long as they are in power. I think that you would be showing disrespect for the high honor that has been conferred on you and me by God.

"Respect everybody, everybody will respect you. This I mean from my heart; everywhere we go respect people and people will respect you. Don't think that you are so great now just because God promised you the kingdom, wait until you get in.

"Again you must remember that by the ruler being dishonorable and dishonoring people: he is dishonoring himself. My beloved brothers and sisters, God does not mean for us to waste our time looking to see who we can make mockery of. Looking and trying to show people up.

"WE MUST SHOW THE WORLD that we are righteous people trying to set up the characteristics of people of righteousness. We don't want our people acting unrighteous regardless to who acts unrighteous to us. We must not do so ourselves since we represent ourselves as being righteous people.

"If we say, there goes the devil, then don't try to fashion after him if you say you're righteous. Show the devil that you are righteous, because he is watching you.

"Let us remember these words, that there is much you must learn to do to show forth to the world who we are. We were not raised up to sit around and make mockery of people; we were raised to show the world what righteousness looks like and what it feels like to be righteous.

"WE MUST REMEMBER that the fault is not in the slave master anymore; since he say you can go free and we say today he is not hindering us, it is we who are hindering ourselves. Give justice to whom it is due. We glorify in making fun and charging the slave master with keeping us a slave; he can't hold you a slave now; you are holding yourself a slave.

"I say to you my beloved brothers and sisters give justice to where it belongs and don't try to rob people out of justice. If the white man, said he has freed you, and he has freed you and me to go to work for self, and you go all around the earth, he doesn't object. You go wherever you want to. And he is not to blame today; you are the one to be blamed.

"THIS IS A VERY SLY and spooky way that we have of dumping the burden on someone else. Right is right and we are of the Nation of righteous. Take our place among the righteous doing right. I love you, but I love you to do something for self and stop putting your fault on the slave-master.

"If you say, "Well, he won't let me do so and so," the earth is big. Go somewhere where you can do something for self without being hindered. Regardless to him trailing us to make it hard for us. But that didn't stop him from opening up a great country that you and I are sitting in here glorifying our freedom.

"WHAT I, AM, saying to you, we cannot put all the fault on the white people. No, he doesn't deserve us charging him with all the fault, because you are free.

"So we must get up and do something for self, seeing nobody is hindering us from doing for self. We must go and do for self and stop charging the old slave-master for being our hindering cause, he is not, it is ourselves.

"Now since you have known self and now you know your once slave-master and he is not trying to hinder you from being yourself, I say be yourself. We all love to be equal with other people who are equal. Well, then, do something to make them to accept us as their equal. We can't set up there on the curbstones and tell him to come and sit down with us, No! We are a lazy people who like something for nothing; that is what we are, lazy.

"WE CANNOT TAKE A country like this and build up cities from one end of it to the other like the white man has done. "Well, we helped him." Well, that was your fault. Certainly he was going to use you if you did not use yourself. He takes our woman, you say, and make a dog out of her. You are not trying to make anything out of her yourself.

"Take her and make them to know that you are intelligent enough and love your woman enough to make something out of her. We are making an example, there they are (pointing to sisters dressed modestly in the balcony).

"HE IS A DESTROYER, You can't ask a destroyer to restore or fix up that which he has destroyed, he is a destroyer.

"Take your woman, restore her back in her "honored" place. Keep her in her place. Don't let him see her running Saturday night —Nope! He didn't tell you to send your woman out there on the street. You did it yourself, and you should have kept her at home —at home where she belongs. And if you don't keep her in your home, naturally, she is acting like a wild beast out here and she is subjected to anybody.

"Look at it now, take your woman off the streets out of the public eye and then the public will respect you. Nowhere do you go and find women with so much freedom as you find in America. They are free to ramble all night long and come home whenever they please, and you are out there looking for them, helping them; they cannot be respected with any such power. We've got to clean up our house and make our people win self-respect then others will respect them and respect you.

"IF YOU WERE UP HERE where I am, you look very beautiful out there. So I say to you that you cannot put on a white dress or a black dress and expect people to respect the dress.

"I am about to discontinue our subject this afternoon. But I want you to remember, if you put on a white dress, clean, spotless and in that dress is unclean, you cannot be respected like that. We cannot go out and tell the public "I am a Muslim," unless we practice the principles of such. We've got to respect and practice the principles of Islam.

"I HAVE VISITED the Muslim World, I have made pilgrimages to Mecca and Medina – and I have seen, and I have heard. These people don't believe in foolishness, so I am trying to clothe you not only with the garments of salvation but clothe you with the principles of our religion. These men are not here to look at you just trying to be Muslims – they are here wanting to know whether or not that you are Muslim at heart. As Salaam Alaikum"

This speech would capsulize his whole mission, outlook, and evolution into proper behavior and conduct into the future. This speech was a call to reality. Don't blame others for our failures. Blame yourself!

His message was the same as great leaders before him: "Up you mighty people you can accomplish what you will."

Honorable Elijah Muhammad Last Savior's Day Address
February 1974

That this would be the last Saviour's Day Public Address by the only leader they had known and looked forward to seeing and hearing at the National Convention that grew out of a house and into the largest public indoor stadium in Chicago with an audience of black and white people.

I was there, sitting on the stage representing the believers of the West Coast when he made that speech. The Honorable Elijah Muhammad was physically weak. He could hardly stand up. He was bending over backward. His security brought a chair on stage and tried to get him to sit down, but he would not. He stood there for nearly two hours delivering his message. When he finished, he walked off the stage as he came on the stage — unassisted.

I was standing at the front of the podium because one member of the security F.O.I had been holding down that postposition too long without relief. After seeing him waver and fall backward, I stood up in his position. The other ministers on stage caught the brother who was falling, while I took his post.

It was historic for me, because the first time that the Honorable Elijah Muhammad spoke outside of Temple #2's property, at the Moslem Convention in February 1957, I stood front post. The last time he spoke, at the Saviour's Day Convention in February 1974, I stood up to stand post for him as well.

That same year (1974), the State of Illinois proclaimed Friday, March 29, as The Honorable Elijah Muhammad Day, presented by Governor Dan Walker of Illinois and Mayor Richard J. Daley of Chicago. This honor was due to his efforts of social reform among African Americans.

In the mayor's proclamation, he cited The Honorable Elijah Muhammad for having "exhibited strong leadership to provide quality education, to create jobs, establish prosperous businesses, organize recreational activities and develop good citizenship in the community."

According to the Chicago Daily News and Chicago Sun-Times Newspapers that covered the event, numbers of leaders across social, business and political spectrums were in attendance for the tribute. A few of these included State Sen. Cecil Partee (D-Chicago), toastmaster; Lt Gov. Neil Hartigan; Aid Wilson Frost (34th), who represented Mayor Daley; State Sen. Charles Chew (D-Chicago); Irwin France, Chicago Model Cities Director; Squire Lance, special assistant to Gov. Walker, and Stanley Scott, special assistant for minority affairs to President Nixon, Muhammad Ali, former heavyweight champion, Floyd McKissick, President of Soul City and Rev. Jesse L. Jackson.

Rev. Jesse L. Jackson, President of Operation PUSH, who presented a plaque for the Honorable Elijah Muhammad, said:

> "This plaque conveyed an appreciation of a Black Muslim Leader, hero, and legend of our own time. The Honorable Elijah Muhammad represented for many persons —a way out of the wilderness. His religion has helped stop men from shooting dope in their veins, and instead has put hope into their brains."

Muhammad Ali, the heavyweight boxing champion, said of Mr. Muhammad,

> "This little black man took me, Cassius Clay, from Louisville, KY, and taught me who I was, and gave me a new name, Muhammad Ali."

Floyd McKissick, President of Soul City, a black real estate development in North Carolina stated, "This man has been first on so many things it embarrasses the rest of us."

I believe this was a just and due honor for a man who neglected himself and put the black man's problems first.

It would be eleven months later, February 25, 1975, that the Honorable Elijah Muhammad died.

Two weeks before he died, I had received a call from the National Secretary, Abass Rassoull, to come to Chicago to help promote the Saviour's Day Convention. Minister Jeremiah Shabazz, leader of Temple #12 in Philadelphia, was also called. We were to work together.

The Honorable Elijah Muhammad had been in Chicago's Mercy Hospital since the last few days of January receiving treatment for his asthmatic-bronchitis condition. Then, according to his grandson and constant companion, Sultan Muhammad, he was rushed to the intensive care unit after being stricken with Congestive Heart Failure.

Minister Jeremiah and I were in full swing responding to request for interviews from many radio and television host. Their concern was the health of the Honorable Elijah Muhammad, the attitudes of thousands of Muslims already in Chicago and its future leadership.

Joining with us the last four days, before the convention on the tour of radio and television station was Minister Wallace D. Mohammed. He told us that he would wait in the car and if needed he would come right in and join us.

Meanwhile, we discovered that the Honorable Elijah Muhammad's condition had gotten worse. Brother Herbert Muhammad, his third oldest son, called Minister Jeremiah and I and asked if we wanted to visit his father in the hospital. Of course, we said yes, and he took us there. Sultan Muhammad, who was Herbert's son, greeted us and introduced us to his grandfather's physician, Dr. Charles Williams.

He gave us a brief update on the Honorable Elijah Muhammad's medical condition and told us that if we go into the intensive care unit don't stay too long. Minister Jeremiah went in first. When he came out, I went into the room. I stood over his bed and prayed for him. He was always thin, but I had never seen him this thin. A month of intravenous feeding will do that to anyone. As I stood there looking upon that frail body, I thought to myself, that body could not carry that tremendous spirit anymore.

Before we left the hospital, Sultan told us that his grandfather became ill when they were in Cuernavaca, Mexico at his home there. He said he awoke one night during a thunder and lightning storm and went into his grandfather's room and he wasn't there. He went looking for him and found him outside in the rain standing by the car. He said his grandfather kept saying over and over, "But I don't understand." So they hurriedly flew him back to Chicago where his physician, Dr. Williams immediately admitted him into Mercy Hospital. That was on the 23rd of February in 1975, two days before our final scheduled news conference at the Pioneers Building on 78th and Cottage Grove Avenue.

At 8:00 O'clock on Saturday morning, February 25, Minister Jeremiah and I were waiting in the conference room of the Pioneers Building for the news conference to begin when the National Secretary Abass Rassoull came into the room. He told us that, "The Honorable Elijah Muhammad had just been pronounced dead by his physician, Dr. Charles Williams, the news conference was canceled." Then he broke down and cried. We left the room in silence. Not disbelief, but in silence, because when we last saw him alive, he was being fed through an intravenous tube and breathing heavily through an oxygen mask. Like all living creatures of God, he completed his mission in this life and moved on. May God forgive him of his errors, hardships and grant him paradise for the good that he did.

That same night, Saturday, February 25, the Honorable Elijah Muhammad's family and the National Laborers of Chicago met at his newly built home and selected a Convention spokesman. Minister Wallace D. Mohammed was selected to deliver the keynote address at the National Guard Armory on Stony Island.

Over 20,000 people assembled in the Armory and an untold listening audience on radio.

All of the regional ministers spoke before Minister Wallace D. Mohammed stepped to the podium and delivered a dynamic and sobering address.

The Regional Ministers presents were: Yusuf Shah, Temple #2, Chicago, IL; Louis Farrakhan, Temple #7, Harlem NY; Abdul Rahman, Temple #15, Atlanta GA; Jeremiah Shabazz, Temple #12, Philadelphia PA; and, myself Abdul Karim Hasan, Temple #27, Los Angeles CA.

In his keynote address, Minister Wallace D. Mohammed said:

> "The Nation of Islam is not this little small black community in America. The Nation of Islam is every Muslim Community that is scattered all over this planet earth."
>
> "We have to take this (the Glorious Quran) down from the shelf. We say we are Muslims. What my father taught that is in this book, we will keep. What is not in this book, we have to give up."

Those of us who were listening attentively that afternoon heard the clarion call for change. Take the Holy Qur'an off the shelf. Read it. Put the message in your heart and live it. A new day is dawning for us, and with a new day comes new knowledge, new experience, and fundamental changes. The evolution of Muhammad Temples into the final evolutionary stage of universal Islam had begun.

Over 20,000 people witnessing this dynamics address by Minister Wallace D. Mohammed overwhelmingly accepted him as the new Muslim leader.

When Minister Wallace Mohammed finished, all the National Laborers and Regional Ministers hoisted him upon their shoulders, saying: "All Praise is due Allah, long live Mohammed."

The next day, Monday, Minister Mohammed met with over 300 ministers from our association who represented Muslims in every state where there was a Temple.

There were 79 numbered Temples and over 200 non-numbered Temples. One of the more memorable things he said to us that day was, this old relic that we call our National (the blackboard depicting the cross and crescent) had to go. It was a good sign that change, and progress in that change, would be constant. Of course, there were those who did not want to change. So, they left with like-minded people, peacefully.

The Honorable Elijah Muhammad left behind the great legacy of an African-American man, who had to quit school in Georgia in the fourth grade to work and help take care of his brothers and sisters.

In a tribute to the Honorable Elijah Muhammad, a 1975 Jet Magazine editorial comment by staff writer Simeon Booker read in part:

> "The Honorable Elijah Muhammad built a kingdom on earth among people who knew little about faith and hope.
>
> "For his multitude, who believed in him and his word, he promised results, not only a salvation of the mind and body, but also a kingdom of thriving businesses. And, there grew nationwide strings of restaurants,

supermarkets, banks, a national newspaper, and schools for the children who many in this country had believed were unable to learn.

"A wise man and master teacher, Muhammad's main message pointed out how blacks can survive in the United States through self-love and self-help."

Dr. C. Eric Lincoln, Chairman of Fisk University's Department of Religious and Philosophical Studies and Author of the book Black Muslims in America, appraised the impact Muhammad had upon blacks, this way:

"Elijah Muhammad gave Blacks new confidence in their potential to become creative and self-sufficient people. In addition, he taught his followers the efficacy and rewards of hard work, fair play, and abstinence. It has been shown beyond a shadow of a doubt that the Muslims who have followed his economic teachings have been comparatively prosperous and have in many cases moved substantially ahead in their economic pursuits."

Father George Clements, Pastor of Chicago's Holy Angeles Roman Catholic Church, whose congregation offered a memorial mass to the Black Muslim Messenger, commented:

"His teachings of dignity, self-respect, discipline and a sense of responsibility are the great works he leaves behind. And, this we admire no matter what our religion."

Chicago's United States Congressman Ralph Metcalfe said succinctly:

> "Mr. Muhammad's life was one of peace, harmony, and great integrity. He made the Nation of Islam a pillar of strength in black communities throughout the country."

The Honorable Elijah Muhammad did not set out to amass a vast mountain of wealth for himself. He wanted to help people find their place in society.

He said that we had been robbed of the knowledge of self. If we were just robbed of wealth, we could acquire more wealth. But, if you are robbed of knowledge of self, you have been robbed of the knowledge of how to acquire wealth.

Plantation life did this to the slave. For three hundred years, teaching the slaves how to read and write was unlawful, punishable by public flogging.

It took the best scientists in the world forty years after the Wright Brothers' crude air flight in Kitty Hawk, NC to learn how to use jet propulsion in air flight.

It took hundreds of years for scientists to build a rocket similar to the Chinese firecracker rockets. And, it only took forty years for The Honorable Elijah Muhammad, a man with very little formal education, born only thirty-two years after Emancipation, to build a community of people whose worth and value in Chicago holdings alone was estimated to have been near $100,000,000.

Following the Honorable Elijah Muhammad's death in 1975, Imam W. Deen Mohammed selected me to assemble a team and take inventory of the holdings of the Nation of Islam.

So myself along with Clyde Rahman, under the direction of Imam Mohammed, took an inventory of all the Nations businesses in and outside of Chicago, Illinois. I had previously been selected to represent Imam Mohammed and the National Community holdings including the Guaranty Bank.

This is only part of what was found, recorded and reported:

Farm Land: 9000 acres in Alabama producing beans, corn, wheat, cotton, vegetables, and watermelons. Over a three-year period, we harvested and transported 1,240,000 pounds of watermelons from 5,000 acres in Georgia.

Main crops: Soybeans, corn, hay, and a beef herd of eight-hundred head. An ultra-modern dairy with two herds of milking cows, as well as a cannery and 1,000 acres of land in Michigan.

Main crops: corn, fifty acres of apple orchards, two huge silos with a 100,000 bushel's capacity, storage bin: two house egg factory containing 40,000 chickens, a dairy herd of one hundred milking cows and Holstein milking cows.

Progressive Land Developers was a holding company that held title to most of the Nation's property—grocery stores, supermarkets, fast food shops, first class three hundred capacity Salaam Restaurant, clothing stores, coffee shops, and bakeries.

Fish markets (cooked and uncooked), and newly built three story Sales and Office building, on Stoney Island in Chicago.

The Nation's Bank, The Guaranty National Bank Recapitalization — I met with State Banking authorities several times.

- American Punch Food — M.R.E — Plant.
- $23,000,000 contract from President Carter's Government
- University of Islam School Building

- Muslim Import Store
- Muhammad Import Warehouse containing imports from Japan: watches, pots and pan, clothes, household goods, fabric, luggage, and tableware, dishes, and utensils.
- The National Clothing Factory, containing uniforms and streetwear for women.
- Several Dry Cleaning Plants,
- Our Truck Fleet, which included three brand new Kenworth tractor & trailer trucks, two brand new Peterbilt tractor and trailer trucks, and one brand new International tractor and trailer truck
- One B-24 Cargo Plane (that crashed on landing)
- One Lear Passenger Jet (sold for $2,000,000).
- Muhammad Speaks Newspaper's brand new $2,000,000 printing press and 60,000 square feet newspaper plant.
- Chicago Lamb Packer Slaughter House, where our meats were slaughtered and prepared for shipping.

There were over two hundred homes and units of housing for over eight hundred people in Chicago. Farming equipment and equipment that if lined up end to end would stretch nearly three miles.

The National communities built Temples in New York (the Malcolm Shabazz Mosque), Washington DC, Kansas City, MO, Oakland, CA, and Los Angeles CA at 5606 Broadway.

There was almost $3,000,000 in cash in the #2 Poor Treasury Bank Account.

But, the jewel was Muhammad's Temple #2, on Stony Island. The $4,400,000 magnificent church building was purported to be one of the ten finest churches in the country. It was too much for us to handle in 1969. The Honorable Elijah Muhammad sent a team of National Laborers to Libya seeking help. The Christians wanted all cash. Muammar Qadafi, the President of Libya, agreed to loan us the money and we bought the church, in addition to five brand new homes on Woodlawn and 48th Street.

The Honorable Elijah Muhammad lived in one of the homes, and when he died, Imam W. Deen Mohammed made it a National House and Museum, where out of town guest could stay. Imam Mohammed never lived there. He only held meetings there.

Nationwide, the decline in our Temple owned businesses began with the appointment of a National Business Advisory Group in Chicago.

The National Laborers were sent to the major Temples to review the financial and ownership records and identify what businesses needed to be jettisoned. They were ordered to mandate the spin-off all Temple owned businesses into the hands of those that worked in them throughout the country.
The Chicago businesses transferred to pioneers who were still functioning and working in the community.

After a review of Temple #27's business portfolio, their findings were that our records were neat, orderly, and our income sheets and payout sheets were factually correct. However, they said that we were not using acceptable accounting methods, although our bottom line was found to be the same as theirs, they made an issue of that.

Nevertheless, we were told to spin-off our businesses. That is what we did. Everything went to those who were working in the businesses: the supermarket, gasoline station, trucks, bakery, fast food, everything!

The mistake that was made, however, in spinning off these businesses cost Temple #27 dearly. We did not close out the Temple's corporate responsibility before we spun the businesses off. Therefore, when that business stopped functioning, the Temple ended up with a tax bill.

The believers at Temple #27 discussed the issue of the enormous tax bill and implemented ideas to raise money to eliminate any liens on the property, owed from businesses that did not pay their taxes.

It would be years later, however, in the mid-80s, that a probate judge decided the second part of the dissolution of the National business interest.

The Honorable Elijah Muhammad died intestate which means he died without making a Will. When a disagreement developed over what was Nation's property as opposed to what was the personal property of the Honorable Elijah Muhammad, some of the children sued the estate.

CHAPTER 10:
Our Community Evolves

During the years of our legal struggles, and from the time Imam Mohammed assumed leadership, following the Honorable Elijah Muhammad's death, we continued to reach out to the outer communities for opportunities to introduce Imam Mohammed new leadership and direction towards universal Islam.

In 1976, at the Los Angeles Sports Arena, we were able to bring together the Jewish, Christian and Singh Dhama faiths with Imam Mohammed to discuss the common issues they share during an Interfaith Dialogue Conference. It was the second of various Inter-Faith Conferences held by Muslims and non-Muslims in America.

Before the Interfaith Dialogue, Imam Mohammed held a press conference. I, using these words, introduced him to a large contingent of Los Angeles news media:

"This is the first news conference held in the western part of America by Imam Wallace D. Mohammed since he assumed leadership of the Nation of Islam, now known as the WORLD COMMUNITY OF AL-ISLAM IN THE WEST. Many changes have been made in the make-up of the Muslim community since he has assumed this leadership. Some of the changes have been minor, some major, but all of the changes are significant and important. Sharing the platform with Imam Wallace D. Mohammed today during the time of the speaking at our Second Annual Spiritual Jubilee will be political leaders and religious leaders representing the Jewish faith, the Christian faith, and the Singh Drama faith. Now, I will present to you, Imam Wallace D. Mohammed who will make a statement and open himself up to your questions. Thank you."

Imam Mohammed, who was sitting behind me, then stood-up, with camera's flashing in his face and addressed the news media:

Imam Mohammed - 1976 Press Conference (Los Angeles, CA)

Imam Mohammed:
"Gentlemen of the press and Imam Hasan, I'd like to thank him for inviting us here today to be guest on this

very special platform with ministers of Christian faith here sharing the platform with Muslims and also Rabbi Jewish representatives and a representative from the Singh movement. I'm especially happy today to be a part of the platform to contribute to the Jubilee's Second Annual Jubilee. Imam Hasan was very much correct when he said that we have brought about real changes in the community, in the world community of Islam, which was known as the Lost Found Nation of Islam under the leadership of The Honorable Elijah Muhammad. Those changes I'm sure most of you are familiar with but at this time I will accept questions from you."

Question:
Especially what are the changes, major changes you are talking about briefly?

Imam Mohammed:
"One of the major changes, I would say the most profound changes that was made, was the change in the belief that G-d is black or manifest in black flesh and that the devil is white or manifest in Caucasian flesh. This was, I believe the most disturbing change, if I can put it that way, the most disturbing change that has taken place. But it has been in accord with the direction, if not with the teachings, of the Honorable Elijah Muhammad. That change is in accord with the direction of the Honorable Elijah Muhammad because he gradually influenced the thinking of the membership in that direction. And it is definitely, as all of you will recognize,

it is definitely in accord with the Qur'an, the Book that the Honorable Elijah Muhammad established in the Nation of Islam as the supreme guide for the organization."

Question:
What is the attitude now towards whites and other races?

Imam Mohammed:
"Well, the attitude in the past, as you know, is one of suspicion and fear. Suspicion suspecting the Caucasian would abuse the trust if they were trusted and a fear that the community wouldn't be able to grow with Caucasians being present. The Honorable Elijah Muhammad felt his work was one of a healing, healing of the minds and the spirits of the Bilalian people or the Black people, and he saw himself as a doctor of the mind and he was digging deep secrets up out of the minds and souls of the Bilalian people and he felt that could best be done in privacy, that is if Caucasians would have been present he felt that would have made his work almost impossible."

Question:
To follow-up if it's not suspicion and fear now, what is the attitude?

Imam Mohammed:
"The attitude now is one of respect and appreciation."

Question:

What are your feelings then toward integration?

Imam Mohammed:

"Integration—Well we hate to think of ourselves as separate or as integrationist. We like to think of ourselves as just human beings."

Question:

Can you give us an idea as to the growth of your particular religious movement in the West? How large It has grown, what your numbers are specifically?

Imam Mohammed:

"During the first year of my leadership, that is during the year 1975 and early 1976, we noticed there was a 100% increase in the membership during that year. In terms of numbers, none of us know the exact number of Muslims that belong to the World Community of Islam. We don't know the number that belong to the old leadership, the Nation of Islam, at it was called. But, we do have a record of what we call workers, those who support programs who belong to a committee, their number now are all over 70,000 people. But if I would give a conservative figure an estimate of the number of Muslims that identify with the old leadership of the Honorable Elijah Muhammad and with the new leadership the World Community of Islam in the West, I would say its well over a million-and-a-half."

Question:
You recently held Independence Day celebrations on the 4th of July, what is your posture towards the American government at this time.

Imam Mohammed:
"Well, the Honorable Elijah Muhammad had always felt that government was an important element in human development, important part of human nature, human growth and he tried to get his people to understand that government was the nature of man, the nature of human society and that it was a spiritual duty or religious duty for us to grow in that direction toward government. So government has always been an aim and object for the World Community of Islam under Elijah Muhammad and when I came into leadership, I saw that the only way we could really realize growth toward government and having government in our lives, in the individual life and in the Community life, I felt that the only way we could reach that would be to identify with the nation or land we live in. And that's America! And the Honorable Elijah Muhammad over a period of 40 years gradually brought us from the idea of going back to Africa to the idea of staying in America and during the last couple of years of his rule among us he led us to accept that we live in America, not just as a separate nation or separate society, but live in America as a people who want to belong to America and contribute something to America. It's not known that widely, but the Honorable Elijah

asked the Fruit of Islam to go out and help a political candidate in Chicago and he secretly made contributions to political candidates. He never asked his people to vote because he felt his people would feel he was betraying them. He felt it wasn't time for his people to identify with the American political system and the government. But in his own long-range plans, his own secret plan, he saw the Community gradually merging in, blending in with the society."

Question:
Many Black leaders express dissatisfaction with the Carter Administration as far as the appointments he's made of Black personnel in his cabinet. Are you equally critical of the President? Are you happy with what you've seen so far as this Administration is concerned as it relates to Blacks in general?

Imam Mohammed:
"Yes, I am"

Question:
In what way? Can you elaborate?

Imam Mohammed
"I won't say I'm pleased or satisfied, but you asked me if I'm happy and I'm happy. Because he represents moral strength and I think what America needs most is moral strength."

Question:

Imam Mohammed, what do you hope to achieve through the Muslim, Christian and Jewish dialogue that you've been having?

Imam Mohammed:

"More oneness, Muslims believe in the oneness of G-d, the oneness of society and we don't believe society can function well unless its in agreement with itself and I see more oneness, more movement towards oneness, accord."

Question:

Recently you were visited in Chicago by the Under Secretary of the World Muslim League of Mecca, Saudi Arabia. I believe you were invited with a contingent of over 300 Muslims to visit Mecca. Does this in any way signal closer ties or closer relationships with Mecca, Saudi Arabia and the rest of the Muslim world?

Imam Mohammed:

"Yes, we now enjoy excellent relations with the Muslim world. With Saudi Arabia with Sheik Harkhan who is the President now of the World Muslim League. With Sheik Bin Bass who is the leading Sheik in Saudi Arabia and with all the Muslim centers."

Question:
What accommodations will be made for that delegation of 300 or more that will go with you there to Saudi Arabia?

Imam Mohammed:
"Well, as an expression of their happiness over us coming into what they call Sunni Islam, which means that we have not only clearly declared ourselves to be not only Muslims, but followers of the Qur'an and followers of Prophet Muhammad. They have shown their happiness over that decision by giving us free land accommodations. That is we pay nothing but transportation and the land accommodations will be free to us."

Question:
One more question Mr. Mohammed. I understand there is a new policy as it relates to the Muslim women. I understand that you have an attack on racism and sexism. Could you elaborate on the new policy that the World Community of Islam has as far as the woman is concerned? What role does she play?

Imam Mohammed:
"Well, the woman in Islam. First, let me explain the development. We began to criticize the treatment of women in the world not just in America, not just in

western society, but in the world even in Muslim lands. We began to criticize it because I feel and know that misreading of scripture has really caused a lot of the misconceptions we have about women. The Bible gives us female figures and these figures are portrayals of a wicked person. Delilah, well even Eve, the first woman Eve and Delilah and Jezebel and all these people and wicked nations are called women. Babylon —the woman —the wicked woman. So it is our feeling that that symbolic language had to be interpreted so that people understand that the Bible is not talking about women as a physical female woman but it's talking about wicked nations who should be mothers to their subjects."

Question:
I have a two-part question. You have refuted the story of Adam and Eve told in the Bible as it is interpreted by the masses. Should we embrace Darwin's history of evolution and can you define life after death?

Imam Mohammed:
"Muslims don't believe in the Darwin theory of evolution, we don't accept the Darwin theory of Evolution. But I would say society is much better off with that theory than with the belief a woman was created with the weak rib of the man. We believe in the evolution of the internal person, that is the evolution of the spiritual person. The mind, the human mind, the human spirit, the soul, we believe that it evolved, stage by stage, until it reaches its fulfillment."

Question:
You've asked for a removal of racial images of Christ. How does that square with you now entering with coalition efforts with Christian-Jewish communities?

Imam Mohammed:
"I think I'm a part of a majority. I'm with a majority of Christians who believe the same. Christians are not displaying Jesus in a physical body as they use too. When I was a child, I saw Jesus on the crosses everywhere as a Caucasian man with blond hair and blue eyes but I hardly see any of those images now. The ones I do see, they look more like a Jew. They have black hair and brown eyes."

Question:
You said that was damaging to the psyche of Black people. What do you mean by that?

Imam Mohammed:
"Well, the colonial world needed racism and the image of a Caucasian G-d to serve that need. Now, America has matured and seen her sins and America wants to be a human nation and not a material power so much, but America wants to be human now as much as it once wanted to be a material power of world dominance and if we are going to have American mind and spirit consistent with American aspirations then we're going to have to put down displaying G-d's son as a Caucasian. If you

display G-d's son as a Caucasian then the mind automatically accepts his father as a Caucasian. We can't think of the son being something different from his father."

Question:
What about the issue of service in the armed forces?

Imam Mohammed:
"Armed forces, well as you know the Honorable Elijah Muhammad was given five years in prison for refusing to go to World War II, to accept to be drafted. Three of his sons and I'm among them, served time in prison for the same thing, for refusing to go to armed services. At the time, the conditions in America, what I mean by that, the race treatment we received in America was so unfair that the Honorable Elijah Muhammad and anyone else who stood up in those days and said why fight for a nation, why fight for a country and a nation that won't respect you as an equal citizen. I think they were justified, and the Honorable Elijah Muhammad did a great job, and his voice was one that deserved to be heard and it was heard, but the thing has changed now. The conditions have changed. America went out with just as much energy and spent wealth to defend the rights of Bilalian people or Black people just as the South had once spent wealth and energy to deprive the Black people of those rights."

Question:

I heard you use the term Bilalian and then seemingly interchanging with Black. I understand that you have raised the point that Black people, as they have been called in America, should take on this name Bilalian and they should drop names, called by your father —slave names? Can you tell us something about Bilalian and Black and why you have chosen this name?

Imam Mohammed:

"The Honorable Elijah Muhammad was taught by Master Fard Muhammad and he was converted to the belief that the real problems for us in our Community is one of a search for identity. The internal person is not settled. The mind is not settled because we don't have an identity with past history, traditions, etc., and the Honorable Elijah Muhammad believed that it was healthy to give the Bilalian people or Black people an identity. So he called us Asiatic Blacks, he called us Muslim, etc., which gave us an identity. Now I feel that, that need still exists for identity and since Bilal was a Black person, he represents our ancestry. He was an Ethiopian, Black person and also a Muslim. So, I think its just natural for people to want to identify with their ancestors, and he is one outstanding ancestor."

Question:
Mr. Mohammed, how would you like the average person today to look at members of your religious movement? How would you like them to think about your people?

Imam Mohammed:
"Well, as they would like to be thought about. I don't know."

Question:
Most Americans, I would venture to guess, have a very unusual perception of the people of Islam, the Muslims in general. It has been a negative one in the past, can you tell me how specifically you might yourself be working to change this since you've been at the helm of your movement for the past two years?

Imam Mohammed:
"Well, we've opened our doors to all people. Where before the doors were closed to all people, except people of African descent. Mexicans, even Africans were not allowed to become members of the Nation of Islam. We opened our doors to all people. We began to identify openly with America. To preach respect for the flag and service to the nation. So these are some of the real changes we have made, and I do want people to know us for having made those changes."

Question:

Mr. Mohammed, you've made a lot of changes in a short time. Have they virtually been made now? Are you going to stay with what you've got now or do you expect more of an evolution as you continue your leadership?

Imam Mohammed:

"I would say most of the big changes have been made and if there are any changes in the future, they should be minor changes. I don't see any great changes being made in the future."

Question:

What is the general response of the Caucasian community in terms of coming in now after such a long period of being taught by your father that they were the devil? What kind of response are you getting? Are they visiting your place of worship? Are they participating at all?

Imam Mohammed:

"Very few Caucasians visit the community. We do have some that have become members in Chicago. We have about half a dozen Caucasian members. There are a few who have become members, but I never expected that we'd have a rush of Caucasians coming to the Masjid. You know the doors of Islam have always been open to the Caucasians, in the East and Arabia, all over and we haven't had a great rush of Caucasian into the Mosque of the world. But things are changing. I understand that a lot of Europeans now are visiting Mosques and identifying with the faith. I don't know whether its material success or not, but things are changing."

Question:
You mentioned that you have one-and-a-half-million followers, is that in the West primarily?

Imam Mohammed:
"In the Western Hemisphere"

Question:
You are going to Saudi Arabia when? When is that visit?

Imam Mohammed:
"It will be during Hajj, that's around November."

Question:
Should we continue to set up our own schools or should we become part of public education?

Imam Mohammed:
"There's just not enough money in private hands to run a good private school. The Catholics have had to give up a lot of their schools because of that. But when we look at the public school system it hurts me that we don't have the money to do it because I believe that private schools could perhaps save the minds of the children."

Question:

Could you describe life after death? Imam Mohammed "You're asking me to describe something I've never seen. You know the Bible says and the Qur'an says of the life that G-d has promised us, after this physical creation is finished, says no eyes have seen, no ears have heard, so that life I am talking about is the spiritual life we develop right here on earth. The symbolic description of what happens here on earth. Nobody knows what is going to happen beyond the spiritual grave. All we know is G-d has promised us a new life, and I hope to get it."

Question:

What do you think about bussing throughout the United States?

Imam Mohammed:

"Bussing, well I don't bus people. Bussing is a big problem. I hope they solve it."

Following the news conference, Imam Mohammed joined the other speakers at the Interfaith Dialogue Conference.

In the early '80s, Imam Mohammed also accepted an invitation to be part of a panel discussion at Duke University.

As part of his opening remarks, Dr. C. Eric Lincoln professor of religious studies at Duke University, a noted scholar and author, and former Chairman of Fisk University of Religious and Philosophical Studies, shared with the audience that while researching the origin of the Nation of Islam, he became friends with Malcolm X and eventually the Honorable Elijah

Mohammed, the leader of the Nation of Islam from 1933 to 1975 and Imam W. Deen Mohammed.

Dr. Lincoln offered the following observations on the evolution of Islam among African Americans:

"The Honorable Elijah Mohammed, whom I had the occasion to know in a very personal way, represented to me a stage in the evolution of Islam in the West, in this country. Why "a stage"? Because there was not available to him any immediate, solid tradition which could have answered the questions about Islam in the way that they can now be answered. And so he had to rely upon his own instincts to a degree. He had to rely upon such fragments about Islam as he could catch, like those, for example, from Noble Drew Ali, who preceded him, or from Marcus Garvey, in his efforts to put together an aspect of the faith that would be viable.

Many of the Africans brought here as slaves were Muslims. When this country was finally settled under the Imperator of the British, it was settled as a Christian country. There were no Muslims. There were no Hindus. There were no anything; only Christians and a very small handful of Jews. As a matter of fact, in the beginning there were no Catholics, either. So from the founding of the country until our present decade, because of our immigration laws and because of our general social policies, there was no way for Islam to gain the kind of foothold in this country which would have lent itself to establishment of a tradition. So black people, white people, green people, whatever, had available to them only the tradition of Christianity. There was an exception......many slaves who were brought to this country were undoubtedly Muslims. When I first began researching my study on the Muslims I could not find very much supportive material. Once the study was out and I had the benefit of criticism from others who were historians then it became clear that what Elijah had said to me long before—which was most of the slaves were Muslims—it became clear to me that at least many of them were Muslim; that the few isolated cases I had found, such as the great mathematician they had down at the University of South Carolina and another Muslim they had who had memorized the Qur'an from the beginning to the end, were not necessarily exceptions. There were many Muslims who were slaves, but, as you know, the slaves were not permitted to practice the religions they brought with them.

As a matter of fact, the first things that the slaves master did was to separate all slaves on account of religious traditions in order to minimize the possibility of a road to an insurrection. He took away the drums, for example, so there could be no communication. He separated those who had the same language, the same religion, the same culture. This meant then that in the practical course of things whatever the religions were that the Africans brought with them, they were soon forgotten, dissipated and disappeared. But as I have found in the repeated evidence in my own studies, once there is a strong tradition of a religion, it never completely disappears. There remains a residual recognition of something that is just waiting to become alive again once the right tone is struck. How Noble Drew Ali, who was an uneducated black man from North Carolina, ever came in contact with Islam I will never know. Nobody else seems to know. But there was something in his mind that he recognized as belonging to an experience that his people had had before. Undoubtedly, the same thing must have been true in the case of

143

the Honorable Elijah Mohammed. But the whole point is this. They had no established traditions, such as for example, the Christians had. Christians had the Church of England as something to depend upon.

Elijah did what he said to me he was doing. He said, "Professor Lincoln, you have to cut the cloak to fit the cloth," which means you have to use what you have in order to get where you want to go. It was also clear to me as a sociologist that the Nation of Islam was not merely a religion, but that it was also a vehicle of social protest. It had economic aspects that were tremendously important at the time. It had political aspects that were tremendously important at the time. And, it did more than any other single movement to bring dignity and ethnic pride to black people in America which must surely have been in Elijah's mind or he would not have taught that. What I'm saying then is that I believe that Mr. Mohammed knew full well that his movement as it then existed was not going to meet the requirements of so-called orthodoxy. But I also found out as my study of the movement continued that the people with whom I was coming into contact with in the Nation of Islam were far more concerned with bread and dignity than they were with orthodoxy.

Okay, so then the evolutionary process, as I see it as an outsider, devolves upon the present leader, Imam W. Deen Mohammed, to do precisely what I think he is trying to do and that is to say, to bring the movement to a level of perfection toward which his father pointed, but just like Moses and the Promised Land, was never quite able to get there."

In response to Dr. Lincoln's comments, Imam Mohammed said,

"I would agree with Dr. Lincoln's observations. But I would like to point this out; that along with that need for a religious experience was a need to have the worldly concerns incorporated in the religion, given sanctions, receive sanctions within the religion. And I think it was the presentation of religion with those concerns, with the material concerns, that accounts for the attraction as well. I know many blacks, or African Americans who were attracted to the Temple, as it was called in those days, to the Temple of Islam, but they were really spiritual people. During the sixties a different breed came in. But the earlier years, the thirties, the forties, fifties, until the revolt of the sixties, during this thirty or so earlier years, during the early history, the people were really to be described as a spiritual body of people. But with the revolt of blacks, the civil revolt, the Temple of Islam offered a strong appeal for those militant blacks; so some of them from the Black Panthers and others began to come into the community. I don't think all of them were religious members of those organizations, but they were people who had been influenced by those organizations. They began to join the community in the sixties, and I believe it was the emphasis on business, business development, business growth, along with black pride that attracted those people to the community.

But now I find since I've become the leader, the people that represented the strength of our community, the people that give us a stable membership are mostly people from those years, those early years. They are the spiritual people, and I find the character is changing now, back to what it was before during the thirty years or so of the Honorable Elijah Mohammed's leadership. And I'm just worried now that maybe they will miss the message

—that there is a balance in our religion; that we have to get involved materially as well as spiritually."

Throughout our evolution, Imam Mohammed continued to teach that message of balance between material and spiritual.

CHAPTER 11:
Our Family's Evolution

Faith is like a family tree, with many limbs, and each participant expresses the idea to emphasize in their communities the commonality of faith, that all leads back to G-d, Our Creator.

Some of the latecomers to America come here speaking in their language, in our presence, knowing that we do not understand what they are saying. Some of us mimic them.

The language culture that we were born in is English. We understand English. We think in English. The question is why do they do this?

Some of them try to shame us into disrespecting and condemning the method used by our former leaders, that Allah (Creator of the Heavens and the Earth) ordained for us.

When Allah says, "Be" or "Kun" in Arabic, he starts the process of a thing or being evolving according to His Plan. When left alone, life finds a way, like a seed buried in dirt and darkness. Left alone, evolution causes it to find a way.

Allah put into the heart of the Honorable Elijah Muhammad (a man with a country school third-grade education and thirty-year Bible student) the desire and "know how" to make his contribution in building a nation within a nation that would eventually become a cohesive Muslim Community.

He never taught us to escape from America. He taught us to believe in Allah and escape from the wicked and evil conditions that existed in America.

After-all, where were we to go? Africa? Pakistan? Arabia? No one would accept us. So, we accepted ourselves and started a new life.

In 1956, the Honorable Elijah Muhammad made a statement in the magazine "The Moslem World and the U.S.A," Special Issue, that read:

"Allah says that He will make a new people out of us."

That statement became a reality for us when Imam Mohammed said in 2006 "we are a new people. We are not the same 'old head scratching colored man' or 'negro' or 'black man or woman' of the past. We are a new people, a new people, that did not have to leave the country of our birth to become new."

What makes us a new people? Action — acting on our spiritual and moral beliefs. We are practicing Muslims.

Our faith and our deeds are in accord with the Holy Qur'an and the demonstrated practice of Prophet Muhammad (Peace and Blessings Be Upon Him).

When we were uprooted by money-hungry merchants of death and sold like cattle, horses and stock animals, we lost everything except the awareness of G-d. And He (G-d) answered our prayers. We were like the old Biblical Story of the Sacred Vessels.

The Sacred Vessels were taken from the Temple of Jerusalem and made a mockery. They were filled with wine and strong drinks — A mockery unto G-d.

Some late comers, before criticizing us, should study their own historic period of jahaliyah which lasted from the time of the construction of the Kaabah, by Prophet Ibrahim and his son Prophet Ishmael (Peace Be Upon Them), until the birth of the Prophet Muhammad (Peace and Blessings Be Upon Him), two thousand years later.

The vices of those societies have destroyed hundreds and millions of people and are still destroying them — legally.

The use of wine, whiskey, beer, gin, vodka, cognac and now, in many states, legalizing marijuana, the scourge of cocaine, crack, heroin and cancer-causing nicotine in cigarettes, cigars, snuff chewing tobacco, cigarillos are destroying the human life.

Allah saved us by making Al-Islam our evolutionary destination, in a way, that we knew not, through the introduction of the Quran in a language we could understand.

Allah says in the Quran; this is "A Book which We have revealed to you (O Muhammad) in order that you might lead humanity out of the depth of darkness into the light, by the leave of their Lord."

That is happening in America continually.

Made in the USA
Lexington, KY
17 October 2019